A BRIEF HISTORY
OF NORWAY

BY

JOHN MIDGAARD

TANUM - NORLI · OSLO

Cover by
Hans Gerhard Sörensen
Maps drawn by Kai Övre

ISBN 82-518-0053-6

Nikolai Olsens trykkeri a.s, Kolbotn

CONTENTS

		Page
Introduction		7
I.	*Prehistoric Norway (before 800 A. D.).*	9
II.	*The Viking Age. A Nordic Migration (circa 800 – 1030).*	13
III.	*The Saga Age. A Period of National Independence (up to 1319).*	
	1. Unification and Christianisation	21
	2. Expansion and Peaceful Growth	31
	3. Civil Wars	36
	4. Medieval Norway at its Height	39
IV.	*Union Period. Decline and Fall (1319 – 1537).*	46
V.	*From Dependence to New Freedom (1537 – 1814).*	
	1. Under the Danish Nobility (1537 – 1660)	52
	2. Under an Absolute Monarch (1660 – 1814)	59
VI.	*The Year 1814.*	
	1. Striving for Freedom	68
	2. Defending Freedom	72
	3. Effecting a Compromise	74
VII.	*Norway in Union with Sweden (1814 – 1905).*	
	1. Depression and Recovery. Defence of the Constitution.	76
	2. Liberalism and Nationalism	79
	3. Foreign Policy. Scandinavianism	83
	4. Economic Progress. Social Changes	88
	5. Norwegian Emigration	91
	6. The Thrane Movement	92
	7. Party Politics. The Constitutional Conflict.	93
	8. The Union Issue 1890 – 1905	98
	9. Cultural Life	105
VIII.	*Independent Norway.*	
	1. The Concession Laws	107
	2. Towards the Welfare State	109
	3. Norway and World War I	110

		Page
4.	Arctic Expansion	112
5.	Norway in the League of Nations	113
6.	Economic and Political Unrest	114
7.	Party Divisions	115
8.	War and Occupation (1940—1945)	118
9.	The Post-War Years.	
	a. Reconstruction and Economic Expansion	130
	b. Defence and Peace Policies	137

Norwegian Kings..................................... 148

Leaders of the Norwegian Government 150

Some Works on Norwegian History in English 152

List of Vignettes 153

INTRODUCTION

Norway is a long, narrow, mountainous strip of land on the north-western edge of the European continent, facing the ocean. The word means the way to the north and may originally have designated the sea-lane along the coast.

This helps to explain one of the main trends in the history of Norway. Her connections with the outside world have always been kept alive, and they have chiefly been maritime connections. Throughout the centuries an exchange of goods, of men, and of ideas has taken place mainly in two directions, towards the west and towards the south. Around the year 1000 A. D. the Christian faith came to Norway from England, but in the later Middle Ages relations with Rome were carried on with Germany as the intermediary. Danish and German influences were long paramount till new connections with the west were formed and steadily grew in importance from the 17th century onward.

Relations with countries lying to the east of Norway have not had nearly the same importance. There has been little intercourse with the arctic provinces of Russia; and the long common frontier with Sweden, mountainous and wood-covered, has been much more of a separating barrier than the sea to the south and west.

To the student of human affairs the history of Norway offers a subject of great interest. We witness the birth of a state, its slow and steady growth, but later we observe its decline and virtual disappearance. Then in modern times the nation is reborn and the state reestablished.

To tell the history of Norway in its relations with the outside world and at the same time describe the peculiar fate of the Norwegian state is the main intention of this little book.

John Midgaard.

I. PREHISTORIC NORWAY
(before 800 A. D.)

For tens of thousands of years, large, thick masses of ice covered northern Europe, just as they do Greenland and Spitzbergen in our own time. There were altogether three glacial periods, and the third period lasted until about 13,000 B. C. Then the ice began to melt as a result of a radical change in the climate, which became warmer. The ice gradually receded, according to geologists by about 400 yards a year. About six thousand years elapsed before the whole of Scandinavia was free of ice.

The melting of the ice made it possible for people to live in Norway. The oldest traces of human activity in the country have been discovered at Komsa in Finnmark[1]) and at Fosna in the Möre area[2]). People made primitive implements of bone, antlers and stone. But only the stone things have been preserved. The people must have lived by hunting and fishing. What race they were or where they came from, we do not know for certain. But they may have come by two ways, either across the Kola Peninsula in northern Russia or by way of Denmark and Sweden from central Europe. An immigration by the latter way would have been fairly easy because Denmark and Sweden were at that time contiguous. As for the date of the Komsa and Fosna civilisation, opinions vary very much, but 9000—8000 B. C. seems to be a probable date for the oldest finds.

Next followed *the early stone age* (5000—3000 B. C.), during which people made coarsely shaped tools and weapons of stone,

[1]) The northernmost part of Norway.
[2]) The north-western corner of South Norway.

mainly axes. They still lived by hunting and fishing, and kept only one domestic animal, the dog. They dwelt in the open air or in mountain caves along the coast and the fjords.

In *the late stone age* (3000—1500 B. C.) a marked step forward took place. People started keeping cattle, and gradually they settled down to till the ground and grow grain, and thus became farmers. They ground their axes and fastened them to a handle, which made them far more efficient both for work and battle. It is generally supposed that these important changes were connected with the invasion of new, warlike tribes ("the battle-axe people"). From this period date the first evidences of artistic skill, the naturalistic rock-engravings of reindeer and fishes. They had a magic aim, that of attracting the animals to places where it was easy to kill or catch them.

The bronze age (1500—500 B. C.) marks a further development af agriculture and permanent settlement, and a perfecting of tools and weapons. Bronze is an alloy of copper and tin. These metals or the ready-made bronze objects had to be imported, and, as Norway could provide very few goods for barter, the use of bronze must have been limited to chieftains and other wealthy people. The bronze finds in our country are therefore rather scarce as compared with those in Denmark and Sweden.

From the bronze age we have rock-engravings of a new type, symbolic or semi-naturalistic figures (sun-dials, wheels, oxen, ships) that must have had some connection with fertility cults as well as with practical work. We can deduce that seafaring played an important part in the life of the people.

About 500 B. C. iron first became known in Norway. The first period of the Iron Age, called *the Celtic Iron Age* (500 B. C. — 0), was a period of decline and reduction in population, probably due to å deterioration in climate. But from the beginning of our era the climate became better again, almost the same as at the present time. The population increased and cultural growth was stimulated by the impact af Roman civilisation. The Scandinavian countries now came into close contact with

10

Bronze age rock carvings of ships. From Borge, Östfold.

the north-western parts of the Roman empire, with which they lived in close neighbourhood. This period is therefore styled *the Roman Iron Age* (0—400 A. D.).

The Roman Empire broke down under the pressure of the Germanic migrations (400—600 A. D.). This period of unrest made itself felt also in Norway. New tribes invaded the country and ruins of local fortresses tell of hostility and armed conflicts.

The migrations ceased, and things gradually settled down in central and western Europe. During the next two centuries (600—800 A. D.) Norway experienced close contact with the Germanic-speaking peoples west and south of the North Sea. This is seen in the ornamental art (wood-carvings), which flourished in the first historic period, *the Viking Age*.

Prehistoric development is reflected in the changing *burial customs*. At first, in the late stone age, people were buried in

11

large collective graves. Only one grave of this type has been found in Norway, east of the Oslo fjord. A little later single graves came into use, perhaps an evidence of belief in a continued existence of the individual after death. The rich supply of grave-goods, including tools, weapons and food, in these graves seems to indicate a materialistic conception of this existence.

From the early bronze age there are preserved large mounds of stone and gravel, containing the dead bodies of chiefs (skeleton-burials). But in the late bronze age a new burial custom grew up. The bodies were burned, and the ashes laid in urns, which were placed in the ground under small mounds (urn-burials or fire-burials). The equipment in these graves is very scanty. This may indicate a more spiritual conception of man and of life after death.

In the Roman Iron Age and onwards both types of burial existed. Near some of the skeleton-burials from this time stand stone monuments, many of them adorned with runic inscriptions.

A special type of burial was the ship-burial, a large mound containing a ship on board of which was placed the dead body of a royal person or a person of the chieftain class. Three ship-burials have been found in Norway, the Tune ship, the Oseberg ship and the Gokstad ship. The two last-mentioned ships date from the first part of the Viking Age (800—900 A. D.). The Tune ship is older, dating from around 600 A. D.

II. THE VIKING AGE
A NORDIC MIGRATION
(circa 800—1030)

The Viking Age was a period of expansion for all the three Nordic peoples, Norwegians, Swedes and Danes. The expansion had partly started even in the preceding centuries. Norwegians had settled in the Shetlands and the Orkneys, and Swedes had set foot on the coasts of Finland and Esthonia. Whether these occupations were peaceful or warlike is difficult to decide. Most probably the motives of the occupants were mixed. For even in the Viking Age plundering and trade went side by side.

However, what distinguished the viking expeditions during the first hundred years was their warlike character. They started as short-lived plundering raids carried out by small groups, more or less moved by a spirit of adventure and greed. But gradually they changed into organised expeditions undertaken by armies and navies under the command of chieftains. And in many cases these expeditions led to conquests and settlements in the foreign countries. It may be supposed that overpopulation in many areas, notably in Western Norway, was a main cause of these expeditions.

The viking expeditions went in two main directions, "the eastern way", eastwards, or "the western way", westwards.

The east-going expeditions were mostly undertaken by Swedes, who sailed across the Baltic and there, among the Slavic population, founded a kingdom called *Gardarike*, with Novgorod and Kiev as the main cities. On the Russian rivers they went southwards down to the Black Sea and came as far as the capital of the East Roman or Byzantine Empire, Constantinople, and from here sailed into the eastern part of the Mediterranean Sea. Some of them came to the Caspian Sea and established contact with the Caliphate of Baghdad. Rich finds of Arabian and Byzantine coins tell of the lively trade between the Orient and the Scandinavian countries in those days.

Many of these vikings entered into the service of the Byzantine emperor as soldiers in his guard ("Varangians"). Several of them became officers, who often undertook expeditions to various Mediterranean countries and came as far west as to Sicily. Some of the Varangians were Norwegians, the most noteworthy of them a half-brother of Saint Olav, *Harald Sigurdson*. He became chief of the Varangians and later on King of Norway (see p. 33).

The west-going expeditions were directed against the British Isles and France, and they were undertaken by Norwegians and Danes. The starting event was the bloody attack on the monastery in the island of Lindisfarne (the "Holy Island") off the coast of Northumberland in 793. Then followed a series of raids on various places in England, Scotland, Ireland and France, all of them Christian countries, and it was above all churches and monasteries that were robbed of their treasures. During the 9th century especially, the Celtic world was exposed to the attacks of Norwegian vikings. They founded kingdoms in Ireland, the most important of them being Dublin, in the Isles of Man and Anglesey, in Wales, the Hebrides and northern Scotland.

In the latter half of the 9th century Norwegian and Danish vikings in England (here called Danes) fought against the King of England, defeated him and succeeded for a time in establishing an independent kingdom in the eastern part of England. It was called the *Danelag*, the land where Danish law ruled (lag = law). King *Alfred the Great* succeeded in restoring English sovereignty over the Danelag, and peaceful relations were established.

14

But one hundred years later new attacks began, now under the leadership of royal princes, Danish as well as Norwegian, who later on became kings. Best known among them are *Svein* of Denmark and *Olav Tryggvason* and *Olav Haraldson* of Norway. In many cases they used the method of blackmailing a city, and acquired large quantities of gold and silver in this way. In 1013 King Svein even conquered England, and his son *Canute the Great* united Denmark and England and for some years also Norway under his rule.

On the continent much fighting took place around the mouth of the Rhine and in the Seine area. Starting in 885, a large viking army of Danes and Norwegians (here called *Normans*) even besieged Paris, demanded a great ransom and did not leave the country until the ransom had been paid. At last they became so troublesome that in 911 a French king found it wisest to purchase peace by ceding to a viking leader called *Rollo*[1]) a fertile province near the mouth of the Seine. Thus arose the Duchy of *Normandy*. The Norman dukes here built up a well organised Christian society, in many ways a model state in its time. Later on they came to play an important part in European history through the kingdom they built in Southern Italy and Sicily, through the conquest of England (1066) and through their leadership in the Crusades.

Some viking expeditions went further south, to Spain and into the Mediterranean as far east as Sicily. Here they met with vikings who had gone the eastern way and taken service with the Byzantine emperor. Thus the circle was completed. The viking expeditions embraced the whole European continent.

In the course of the 10th century trade became the dominating element in the expeditions. The states in Western Europe were gradually consolidated, and the Scandinavian countries themselves emerged as national states willing to have peaceful intercourse with other states, including the kingdoms founded by the vikings.

[1]) Whether he was a Dane or a Norwegian is a matter of dispute.

Thus the ways opened up by the warlike expeditions became trade routes which helped to bind together the vast territory of Scandinavian colonisation commercially, if not politically.

However, the viking spirit was not extinct. From about 980 it flared up again, and displayed itself with much of the old intensity. But it was only for a brief period. A new age was now approaching, in which wars between states took the place of private enterprise, and it often happened that the vikings sold their services to a foreign king. This meant the beginning of the end of the true viking expeditions.

The Viking Age had also seen an expansion of a purely peaceful type. This partly took the form of trading expeditions northwards along the coast of Norway and then eastwards as far as the White Sea, and partly of emigrant expeditions westwards to Iceland and Greenland. From around 870 onwards people from Western Norway began to emigrate to Iceland, and in 930 they organised a state by establishing the *Allting*, a body which had legislative and judicial authority.

One hundred years later a man called *Erik the Red* was outlawed in Norway for some crime. He first fled to Iceland, and, after he got into trouble there too, left and settled on the west coast of Greenland. Soon several other Icelanders and Norwegians followed his example. In the course of time two settlements grew up in Greenland numbering three to four thousand inhabitants. More famous than Erik became his son, *Leiv Erikson*, who in the year 1002 came to a land which he called *"Vinland the Good"*. This must have been somewhere on the east coast of North America between Labrador and Virginia, but the exact location was for a long time a matter of dispute. Recent research, however, seems to point to Newfoundland as the most probable place.

Leiv's expedition was followed by others, and there was regular contact between Greenland and Vinland until the middle of the 14th century, mainly owing to the need of the Greenlanders for timber. It seems that even a settlement took place. Gradually

16

also the contact between Greenland and Norway ceased, and at the end of the 15th century the Norwegian population there died out.

A Norwegian expert writes (1962):

"Greenland being geographically part of North America, the medieval Norse inhabitants there could not possibly avoid discovering other parts of North America as well. During the first immigration into Greenland certain parts of Canada were seen by the crew of a ship that sailed off course and missed Greenland on the way out there. These lands seen to the south-west of Greenland were later deliberately explored, the Greenlanders making several voyages told of in two medieval sagas.

The sagas differ somewhat, but by letting them complement each other, and by cutting out exaggerations, day-dreams and fairy tales, the route and extent of the different voyages may be traced with some reliability.

The route of the first explorer, Leiv Erikson, may have taken him to the southern part of Baffin Land, along the coast of Labrador to Belle Isle and down the west coast of Newfoundland (Vinland, i.e. meadow-land) probably to St. George's Bay and up the river to Grand Lake, where a winter camp was constructed.

From here Thorvald Erikson later on proceeded to explore the coast to the south and east, most likely as far as Burin Peninsula and Great Miquelon. Thorvald also began the exploration of northern Newfoundland, rounding Cape Bould and probably reaching Cape St. John.

The serious attempt to colonise made by Thorfinn Karlsevne some time later seems to have gone farther to the north-east of Newfoundland, to Fogo Island and Sir Charles Hamilton Sound. From this base expeditions were extended along the coast both east and west to Cape Ray.

The Vinland voyages mentioned in the sagas have scarcely extended farther than along Labrador and around Newfoundland, but it is possible, of course, that the old Norsemen may have sailed further south on some of their expeditions, though these are not recorded in the sagas."[1]

[1] From an essay by *Leif Löberg* in "Norsk Historisk Tidsskrift" (Norwegian Historical Review), vol. 41 (1961—62), English Summary pp. 251—252.

Excavations made in Newfoundland during the summer of 1962 by the explorer *Helge Ingstad* and his wife seem to corroborate fully the view referred to above. Well-preserved remnants of a Norse settlement were found in the northernmost part of Newfoundland. Certain other findings indicate that the old Norsemen may have extended their expeditions as far south as Rhode Island.

The effects of the viking expeditions on the conquered European populations, apart from all the destruction and suffering they caused, were beneficial in many ways. In many countries the vikings established a rule of law and order which had till then been unknown, for instance in Ireland and Normandy. In England the art of shipbuilding and sailing had been forgotten, but from their viking enemies the English learnt it anew, and the foundation was laid of a British navy.

On the other hand the vikings received powerful impressions and stimuli in the foreign countries. These countries had reached a higher level of material and spiritual culture than the Scandinavian countries. The Irish, for instance, had produced excellent works of ornamental art, which no doubt impressed the Norsemen and influenced their own work in the same field. In England, France, Spain and the Orient they saw cities far larger and more glorious than their own small and poor towns. They became acquainted with new articles of food and new types of cloth (scarlet, silk and cotton) and the use of coins. All this gave great stimulus to trade. *Tunsberg*, according to the sagas the oldest of the existing Norwegian towns, arose in the 9th century.

Something quite new to the vikings was the churches and monasteries, bearing witness of a religious belief and of ideas of good and evil totally different from their own. In spite of their plunder they cannot but have been impressed at least by the beauty and solemn atmosphere of the churches.

Of the Christian religion the vikings may have acquired some fragmentary knowledge even in the 9th century. The Asa mythology was shaped in this period and on the whole reflects the

18

Viking ship found in 1904 in a burial mound at Oseberg, Vestfold, now in the Viking Ship Museum at Bygdøy in Oslo.

viking ideals: the will to fight, courage, and valour. The chief gods were *Odin*, the god of war and wisdom, *Thor*, the god of good crops, an ardent slayer of trolls and giants, and *Tyr*, the bravest and most courageous fighter among them. The gods were worshipped in temples called *hov* or *horg*.

But in the Asa mythology there are also certain traits that may have been inspired by Christian ideas, such as the story of the bright and good god *Balder* and the bad half-god *Loke*, the final doom (*ragnarok*) and the new earth. During the more peaceful period of the 10th century many acquired a better knowledge of Christianity, and those who settled in the viking king-

19

doms mostly became Christians. Among the vikings who were still fighting, many lost their belief in the heathen gods and only trusted in their own "might and main" (power and strength). But this was often a transition to conversion. In the last great period of viking activity (around 1000 A. D.) several of the princely viking leaders received Christian baptism and then turned their energy in other directions. This was the case with two members of the royal stock of Norway, *Olav Tryggvason* and *Olav Haraldson*. They returned to their native country, bent on claiming the throne and forcing Christianity upon the Norwegian people.

This marked the end of the Viking Age.

III. THE SAGA AGE
A PERIOD OF NATIONAL INDEPENDENCE
(Up to 1319)

1. *Unification and Christianisation.*

The Viking Age saw the development of two very important changes in Norway, the political unification of the country and the adoption of Christianity as the official religion of the nation.

Up to the end of the 9th century Norway was split up into a number of principalities of varying size. Their rulers bore the titles of *count*, ('herse'), *earl* or *king*. In spite of the political division, the idea of a geographical whole was alive, and the country was given the name of *Norðvegr* i. e. the northern way, most probably by seafarers sailing along the coast.

In the years before 900 A. D. the unification was carried out by King *Harald*, later surnamed *Fairhair*. He was a local king in the Oslo fjord region, in the saga period called the *Vik*. He belonged to the family of the Ynglings, who according to tradition had come from Uppsala in Sweden and had established their rule over *Vestfold*, the district west of the Oslo fjord. Harald's father had extended his domain to other parts of East Norway and probably also to the *Sognefjord* area, on the west coast. Evidently Harald must have been a man of viking spirit, though his ambition was directed not towards foreign lands but towards the conquest of all Norway.

At the head of an army he undertook a military expedition northwards across the Dovre mountains into the Trondheim area, which at that time belonged to the earls of North Norway (*Haalogaland*). *Haakon Grjotgardson*, the earl then in power, seems to have submitted to Harald's superior force, made an agreement with him and accepted his overlordship. Earl Haakon then took up his abode at the estate of *Lade* (now in the city of Trondheim), where his descendants resided for several generations and became known in history as the Lade earls. They formed a powerful local dynasty. At first they were loyal to the national kings of the Fairhair stock, but later on they became their rivals.

Earl Haakon's example was followed by the neighbouring Earl of Möre. But the local rulers farther south on the western and southernmost coast put up a stiff resistance to Harald's claim. They united their forces and met him in the little bay of *Hafrsfjord*, south of the present city of Stavanger. Here in a naval battle Harald gained a complete victory over his enemies. From that day Harald Fairhair was King of all Norway. Soon afterwards he undertook an expedition to the *Shetlands* and the *Orkneys* and established a nominal sovereignty over them.

After his victory Harald took up his main abode in West Norway, probably to have these rather unruly regions, the bases of many viking raids, under his control. But accompanied by his life-guard ("hird"), he often moved from place to place living at the "royal farms", i.e. lands which Harald had taken from his chief opponents and made his property. Thus the King had become the greatest landowner of the country, a fact which enabled him to keep an armed force at his disposal. This formed the basis of the King's power and made it possible for him to keep the nation united in a fashion. Otherwise the unification was rather loose, there was no national administration and no civil service as yet. The unification, in fact, only meant an internal pacification and the establishment of a primitive military defence against aggression from abroad. According to tradition Harald imposed a general tax, which probably implied that he claimed contributions in kind for the maintenance of himself and his hird when they travelled about the country.

Harald Fairhair is described as a firm and hard ruler. He forbade internal feuds and claimed strict obedience to his commands. Those who disobeyed were either killed or expelled from the country. It is told in the sagas that many found his tyranny so intolerable that they preferred to leave the country and go westwards over the sea or eastwards over the mountain range that to-day separates Norway from Sweden. Here they settled in the district of *Jemtland*, which at that time was an independent republic.

The next period of Norwegian history, down to the year 1319, is called the saga period, because it is described in the Old Norse historical sagas (chronicles), above all in the brilliant saga-book composed by the Icelander *Snorre Sturlason.*

Two tendencies dominate this period, on the one hand a gradual consolidation of political unity and national independence, and on the other a growing cultural contact with Europe, especially after the acceptance of Christianity about the year 1000 A. D.

The work of Harald Fairhair was exposed to dangers from within and without. After his death (ca. 940) his many sons ruled as local princes, although one of them, *Erik* (nick-named *Blood-Axe*), was formally acknowledged as King of the nation. There was much trouble and killing among them. From without the danger came from the Danish kings, who in former days had ruled parts of the Vik area and now showed a mind to get the whole of Norway under their control. Support from discontented elements in Norway gave them increased chances in this respect.

Harald's youngest son, *Haakon,* managed to unite most of the country again and defend its independence against the united aggressions of rival nephews and Danes. Haakon had been educated in England, at the court of King *Athelstan,* and here he had embraced Christianity. When he became King of Norway, he made an attempt at christianising the nation, but met with such a stubborn opposition that he dropped his plan.

But in two other fields he was very successful. He established a naval defence and effected an important reform in the judicial system. At least the sagas ascribe these feats to Haakon,

23

although probably they are partly earlier and partly later than his time.

For defence purposes the coastal regions were divided into districts, each of which had to place a ship fully manned and equipped at the king's disposal for a certain term every year, and a system of warning by means of bonfires on the mountain peaks was established; in the course of seven days the warnings went all over the country. This defence arrangement was called *the leidang.*

From of old the free men had been accustomed to meet regularly at local courts (*tings*) to pass sentences and settle disputes. The achievement attributed to Haakon was the organisation of courts of appeal (*lagtings*) covering larger districts, three in all, a fourth being added later on. These courts were composed of elected men and had not only judicial, but also legislative power.

It is a testimony of Haakon's popularity that he was called *Haakon the Good.* He fell in a battle against his nephews, the sons of Erik Blood-Axe. Their mother was a Danish princess, and they were assisted by the Danes. Before his death Haakon bequeathed the country to his nephews.

Now followed a period of partial dependence on Denmark, in which the national unity was breaking up. At last one of the Lade earls, *Haakon,* succeeded with the help of the Danish king in uniting the greater part of the country under his rule. To begin with Earl Haakon of Lade was dependent on the Danish king, but self-willed and strong as he was, he soon rid himself of the Danish supremacy. When the Danish king sent a fleet with his best warriors up to Norway to force the Earl into submission, he suffered a complete defeat.

After this triumph Haakon developed more and more into a reckless tyrant, says the saga. At last a revolt broke out against him in his home region, the Trondheim area, and during this he was killed (995).

Just at this time a young viking prince of the Fairhair stock, a great grandson of Harald Fairhair, landed in Norway to claim the throne he thought himself entitled to. This man was *Olav Tryggvason* (Olav I), son of a local king in south-eastern Norway.

Olav had had a rather troubled boyhood and youth, having been forced to flee from the country together with his mother after his father had been killed. For a time they lived in Gardarike (Russia). When he grew up, he followed the example of other ambitious young princes and nobles, and went on viking expeditions. First he plundered the Baltic regions, then the Netherlands, and, lastly, England and other parts of the British Isles. Here he fought for many years, sometimes together with the Danish king, Svein. He ravaged and plundered or exacted large ransoms, which made him a very wealthy man. After he had been bought off by the English king a second time, he was finally confirmed in the Christian faith by the Bishop of Winchester. Then he left England and gave up his viking life for good.

In Norway he was at once accepted as King of Norway by the people of the Trondheim area and gradually by the rest of the nation. Thus he restored national unity and independence. His next aim was to make people adopt the Christian religion, and this task he fulfilled in the course of his brief reign of five years, assisted by English missionaries. It was, indeed, an enforcement of Christianity he effected. Whereever he met with resistance, he did not shrink from using threats and even torture to force people to submit to baptism and bow to the White Christ. The official worship of the heathen gods was forbidden and their temples were destroyed. In their place came churches, the first of which were built by Olav Tryggvason.

Olav was a typical viking, physically and mentally strong, an athlete and a sportsman. Evidently he must have appealed very much to the Norwegians of his day and he left a powerful impression on the national mind. In tradition he lived long as the prototype of a national hero.

His death no doubt contributed to the creation of this tradition. Olav had made many enemies for himself through the hardness he evinced in enforcing Christianity. This was especially the

25

case in the Trondheim area, where he set up his abode and founded the city of *Trondheim* (later on called *Nidaros*). The resentment harboured by many of the farmers here fed the ambitions of the two sons of Earl Haakon of Lade, who wanted to revenge their father and get into power themselves. They made an alliance with the Kings of Denmark and Sweden, who both planned to take parts of south-eastern Norway. Olav met their combined forces in the naval battle of *Svolder*[1]). As he had been deserted by a great part of the leidang fleet, he was hopelessly outnumbered, and, seeing the battle was lost, he jumped overboard and was drowned. This battle took place in the year 1000 A.D., the first certain date in Norwegian history.

After Olav's death followed a period of national, political and religious reaction. Norway was once more dependent on foreign kings. The political unity was broken, as the Lade earls controlled only part of the country, and heathen worship again flourished. But in the year 1015 another descendant of Harald Fairhair, one generation younger than Olav Tryggvason, appeared on the scene and turned the tides of fortune. His name was *Olav Haraldson* (Olav II), better known in history as *Olav the Saint* (Saint Olav), the greatest name in Norwegian history.

Olav, born in 995, was the son of a local king west of the Oslo fjord. While still a boy he lost his father, and his mother then married Sigurd, a local king in Ringerike, a district north-west of the Oslo fjord. Here Olav was brought up. Even as a child he showed many of the qualities that distinguished him in his manhood, physical strength, ambition and a strong will.

In his boyhood viking expeditions were still taking place, and the idea that some experience as a viking formed part of the education of an ambitious young man of the chieftain class had not disappeared. At a very early age, therefore, and accompanied by experienced men, Olav undertook viking expeditions to the Baltic regions, and later on he went to western Europe, notably

[1]) The location of this place is uncertain. It is supposed to have been in the Danish Sound or in the Baltic near the island of Rügen.

to England. Here he won great renown as a warrior and also acquired great wealth.

Olav Haraldson was the last great viking chief, but it is characteristic of the new developments in western Europe that most of the time he was in the service of some king, among them the King of England, whom he helped against the Danes. The period of the traditional viking expeditions had come to an end, the time of wars between states had begun. For a long time Olav also stayed in Normandy, and here he became acquainted with the excellent administration of this country, and it was also heer he was converted to the Christian religion.

Soon afterwards he received news that the elder of the two Lade earls had left Norway and joined the Danish king to assist him in subjecting England. The rule of Norway he had left to his brother and a young son. In this situation Olav saw a chance of winning Norway which he, like Olav Tryggvason, regarded as his lawful heritage. So he returned to his native country, and in the course of a year succeeded in establishing his rule all over Norway.

It goes without saying that Olav II's assumption of power was regarded with ill-will by the Kings of Denmark and Sweden. But the Danish king was at that time busy in England, and with the Swedish king Olav later on made friendship and married his daughter. Common fear of a Danish supremacy tied them together.

Olav Haraldson may justly be called the second founder of the Norwegian state. He resumed and completed Harald Fairhair's work by delivering Norway from foreign control and incorporating in the kingdom the interior parts of East Norway, which had till then been rather independent under local kings, and the Vik area, which had partly been under Danish control.

The unification he cemented by means of a feudal system of administration, on the model of that of Normandy. The heads of the big farming families entered into his service as *vassals* ("lendmenn"). In this capacity they undertook to support the king's authority in their several districts and to serve him in the event of war. As compensation for this they received the revenues of royal farms and shares of the fines inflicted by the courts of justice.

Finally he finished the work of christianisation by extending it to the whole country and by doing away with all remnants of pagan worship. Often he used force and cruelty, as Olav I did. Then he set about organising the Church with the assistance of clergymen he had brought with him from England. The king was made the head of the Church, and he was in ecclesiastical matters to be assisted and advised by a national bishop, appointed by him. All regulations relating to the Church and the clergy were embodied in an Ecclesiastical Act, passed by a national meeting ("riksting") in 1024. Like the Churches of Denmark and Sweden the Church of Norway was placed under the supervision of the Archbishop of *Bremen*.

Otherwise the old laws remained in force, but Olav saw to it that they were strictly obeyed by all, and criminals were punished regardless of rank or wealth. This was the reason why the old laws in later times were, wrongly, referred to as "King Olav's law".

All this was in harmony with the will of the people at large. King Olav's rule was accepted and appreciated all over the country. For several years, therefore, all went well. But gradually there grew up an opposition, which to some extent was due to certain traits in Olav's character. He was a dynamic personality who wanted to have his own way, and he was impatient of contradiction and disobedience. It appears from the sagas that he was of a rather irascible temper.

The leading men in the opposition were a group of powerful individuals, who were descended from the hereditary local chiefs and, moreover, were more or less connected with the Lade dynasty through family ties and friendship. They were not unwilling to acknowledge a foreign king as ruler in case an opportunity should offer itself. For they thought a more remote king

Medieval stave church at Borgund.

would be less oppressive to their own power than Olav was. King Canute of Denmark was the man they had in view and he made contact with them by means of secret messengers.

The opportunity came in connection with Olav's foreign policy. In alliance with the Swedish king he attacked Canute and defeated him in a naval battle on the coast of Scania, but the victory was not decisive. After the battle Olav was deserted by the Swedes, his fleet was blocked up in the Baltic, and he had to make his way home by land.

After this, open revolt broke out against him, and the revolt ghaterep strength after one of Olav's men by mistake had killed his most powerful opponent, *Erling Skjalgson*, who resided at Sola in south-western Norway. Still King Olav held his own for some time. But when in 1028 King Canute came to Norway at the head of a large fleet, Olav had to flee from the country, only accompanied by a few faithful followers. He went to Gardarike (Russia), whose grand prince was his brother-in-law, married to a sister of Olav's queen. Meanwhile Canute had been acknowledged as King of Norway, and he appointed a Lade earl as his regent.

Two years later the regent was drowned on a voyage to England. When Olav learned this, he decided to attempt to win back his kingdom. He set off from Gardarike, came to Sweden, where he gathered round him a rather heterogeneous body of Norwegians and Swedes, and marched with them across the Norwegian border into the valley of Verdal in the Trondheim area. Here at a farm called *Stiklestad* he was met by an army of Trondheim farmers, twice as big as his own, under the command of some of his leading adversaries. In this battle King Olav was killed on July 29, 1030. His body was secretly carried to the city of Trondheim and buried in the sandbank of the river flowing by.

Olav's defeat was complete and his cause seemed to be hopelessly lost. But even in the hour of defeat signs of his coming victory began to manifest themselves. Shortly after his death many stories were told of miracles taking place at his grave. Only one year later his body was dug up and placed above the high altar of St. Clement's church as the earthly remains of an acknowledged saint. A radical change had taken place in the feeling of the nation. People now looked upon Olav as a martyr and a champion of national liberty. It was now he became *Saint Olav* and it was not long before he was a national saint uniting the whole people.

The background of this change was a gradually increasing discontent with the Danish rulers whom Canute had installed.

They were used to a greater power for the King, and so imposed rather hard taxes to procure the necessary revenues. Especially the chiefs of the Trondheim area felt greatly irritated at this, for they had expected something quite different. Four years after the battle of Stiklestad two of them went to Gardarike (Russia), where Olav had left a young son called *Magnus*. Next year, after King Canute had died, they brought him back to Norway. The foreign rulers fled from the country, and Magnus was accepted as king without any opposition (1035). This was a national triumph for the deceased King Olav.

Before long Saint Olav received adoration all over Europe and was even acknowledged as a saint in Constantinople. Churches and shrines were built in his honour by the hundred, in Norway as well as in other countries, as far away as in Rome. In London there were no less than six churches dedicated to St. Olav, and several other English churches bore his name.

The centre of the worship of St. Olav was naturally the city of Trondheim. His shrine here attracted every year vast crowds of pilgrims not only from all parts of Norway, but also from foreign countries. The day of Olav's death, July 29, became a great religious festival. His shrine was in the latter half of the century moved to a new church built over his burial place, and this church was later on replaced by the glorious *cathedral* that was built partly on the model of Lincoln Cathedral, and was finished around 1300. On the high altar of this cathedral was placed St. Olav's shrine.

2. *Expansion and Peaceful Growth.*

From now on Norway had the position of an independent sovereign kingdom, acknowledged by the Scandinavian neighbours as well as by other countries. She made treaties and alliances with other nations as equals. Her kings had a definite foreign policy, often rather aggressive, for in some of them the viking spirit was still alive. Thus in the course of time was built up a greater Norway, a Norwegian empire, including the "western islands", i.e. the Faroes, the Shetlands, the Orkneys, the Hebrides and Man, and finally also Iceland and Greenland (in 1261—62).

In Norway itself the period is marked materially by a growing prosperity, owing to the cultivation of new tracts of land, especially in East Norway, and an increased trade, inland and with foreign countries. This led to the rise of new cities (*Oslo, Bergen, Stavanger*) and stimulated the growth of the older ones, Tunsberg and Trondheim. Intellectually there was a development that more and more made Norway an integral part of medieval Europe and its Christian civilisation. Very important in this respect was the improved organisation of the Church. The country was divided into bishoprics, altogether five, each with a bishop's see as its centre: Nidaros (Trondheim)[1]), Oslo, Bergen, Stavanger and Hamar. The bishops soon started building big stone churches (Christ churches or cathedrals) in their sees. The building of churches and monasteries created a many-sided activity, and so did the economical administration of the Church as it grew rich in property and revenue. Both the religious and the financial activity of the Church stimulated the growth of the cities. Also in the western islands and in Iceland and Greenland bishoprics were set up and new churches were built, some of them large, such as the imposing cathedral at Kirkwall in the Orkneys.

The ecclesiastical development terminated in the establishment of an archbishop's see at Nidaros in the year 1153 (or 1152). On this occasion the Pope sent as his legate the English-born Cardinal Nicholas Brekespear.[2]) From that time Norway and its dependencies formed a separate diocese or church province under the Archbishop of Nidaros. And during the centuries that followed the Archbishop came to play a leading part not only in the ecclesiastical but also in the political history of the country.

Magnus the Good (1035—47) started his reign by being rather harsh to the opponents of his father. But on the advice of one of

[1]) The bishop's see was called Nidaros and is called so to-day too.
[2]) A few years afterwards he was elected Pope under the name of Adrian IV, the first and so far the only Englishman to sit in St. Peter's chair.

his skalds or poets[1]) he altered his conduct and soon acquired the surname he bears in Norwegian history.

Adispute with the king of Denmark (a son of Canute) ended in an agreement deciding that the one of them who survived should inherit the other's throne. In consequence of this Magnus became king of Denmark some years later.

Denmark was at that time threatened with invasion by the *Wends*, a heathen Slav people, who were pushing westwards from their homes on the southern shore of the Baltic. Magnus, at the head of a Danish-Norwegian army, defeated the Wends completely and thus put an end to the Slav expansion in this region. In his later years Magnus had some trouble with a nephew of King Canute, who aspired to the Danish throne, and on an expedition against him Magnus died.

His successor, *Harald Hardrade* (1047—66) is identical with the Varangian chief Harald Sigurdson and was a half-brother of St. Olav. At the age of 15 he had fought on Olav's side at Stiklestad, where he was wounded. After the battle he had to flee from the country, and naturally sought refuge in Garda-rike (Russia). Here he stayed for some years and served in the army against Poles and Wends. Next he went to Constantinople at the head of 500 men and was made chief of the imperial guard. As a leader in war he distinguished himself greatly and also acquired a large quantity of gold. He may be regarded as a be-lated viking.

After a brief stay in Russia he returned to Norway, where King Magnus accepted him as fellow-king on condition that Harald shared his gold with him. When Magnus died one year later, leaving no son, Harald became king.

Harald looked upon himself as the rightful heir also to the Danish throne after Magnus. For several years he waged war

[1]) It was customary for a king to have poets called skalds attached to his court. They not only made poems in honour of the king but also advised him. The skaldic poems are regarded as very valuable historical sources.

to win Denmark, but towards the end of his reign he made peace and left Denmark to Canute's nephew. Like Magnus Harald regarded England as part of his heritage after Canute's son. When, therefore, in 1066 rivalries developed between two pretenders to the English throne, he saw a chance of gaining supremacy over England by helping one of them into power. But at the battle of *Stamford Bridge* in Yorkshire he was defeated and killed. Thus this warlike king failed to reach his ambitious aim of reestablishing King Canute's great realm. He had to be content with a limited extension of Norwegian domination by linking the Faroe Islands and the Shetlands more firmly with Norway than they had been before.

Harald Hardrade (Hard Ruler) is the name this king bears in Norwegian history. The name does not necessarily imply cruelty, it is more meant to characterise him as a firm, strong and resolute ruler, who would put up with no rebellious tendencies. Some such tendencies really appeared, especially among the kinsmen of the late Lade earls. The rebels were either killed or had to leave the country.

Harald is also remembered in Norwegian history as the founder of the city of *Oslo*, the present capital of the country, an event which is supposed to have taken place in the year 1048. Here he began building a church, St. Mary's Church, in which the body of the saint of East Norway, *St. Hallvard*, was enshrined.[1] Later on it was placed in the cathedral of Oslo, built in the next century and named after St. Hallvard. Hallvard became the patron saint of the city and his martyrdom is still depicted in the seal of Oslo.

The reign of Harald's successor *Olav the Peaceful* was, as the name indicates, a period of quiet and peaceful growth. It is characteristic that in Snorre's saga-book Olav's reign only occupies three pages. One of the most remarkable features of the period was the improved organisation of the Church. It was now that the

[1] Hallvard was a young man who was killed when trying to save a woman from her pursuers.

division into bishoprics began, and one of the bishop's sees was the city of *Bergen*, which according to the saga tradition had been founded by Olav, about the year 1070. West Norway had by then also got its local saint, *Sancta Sunniva*, an Irish princess who had fled to Norway to avoid marrying a heathen prince. Her shrine was moved from the island of *Selje*, where she had landed and had died, to Bergen.

The city of Bergen became the trading centre of West Norway and in the course of time developed into the biggest city not only of Norway, but of all the Scandinavian countries. It was above all the export of dried fish from West and North Norway that formed the basis of this development.

Olav's son, *Magnus Bareleg*, (so called because he wore a kilt), was more like his grandfather. He preferred a short life full of adventure and fighting to a long life in peace. During his short reign of ten years (1093—1103) he completed his grandfather's work of bringing the western islands under Norwegian rule by finally subjecting the *Orkneys*, and he added the *Hebrides* and *Man* to the Norwegian empire. For a time he also had possession of Dublin, and it was on an expedition to Ireland that he was killed.

His sons *Eystein* and *Sigurd* (The "Brother Kings") were in reality both of them peace-loving kings, who did much to promote material welfare and strengthen the power of law and justice in the country. Thus it was during their reign that the old laws were recorded, in the Old Norse language, but with use of the Latin alphabet. The Church was given a solid financial basis by the introduction of the *tithe* (a ten per cent duty, first on grain, later on all products). Furthermore a limited right of giving legacies was established, and thanks to this the Church in the course of time became possessed of a large amount of landed property.

There is a tradition contrasting a warlike Sigurd and a peaceful Eystein. This is unhistorical, but no doubt based on a historical fact, Sigurd's crusade to the Holy Land between the years 1108 and 1111, shortly after the first crusade. The expedition gave him great renown in his own time and long afterwards, and acquired for him the name of *Sigurd the Crusader*.

Snorre gives a detailed and vivid description of the expedition and of the fighting against the Moslems not only in Palestine, but also in Spain and Sicily. On his home voyage he came to Constantinople, where he was received with great celebration and could display much pomp himself thanks to the rich plunder he brought with him. His crusade was, indeed, a viking expedition on a new basis.

3. *Civil Wars (1130—1240)*.

To understand this part of Norwegian history it must be borne in mind that the monarchy of Norway was of a peculiar type. It was, indeed, a combination of hereditary and elective monarchy. The principle of heredity applied to the stock or kindred. The throne was hereditary in the Fairhair stock, but there was no fixed order of succession. All sons of a king, whether born in marriage or not, had an equal right to the throne. It was the privilege of the local tings (the lagtings) to acknowledge any one of them. Up to now this had caused little trouble. Generally there had been only one king at a time. Sometimes, however, there had been two or even three kings, but they had shared power and ruled in harmony.

After 1130 this harmony was replaced by a state of confusion and bitter strife. From time to time there appeared new pretenders to the throne claiming to be the sons of this or that king. They won supporters among the leading men, who formed factions and took advantage of social discontent (tenants and small farmers versus big landowners) or local antagonism (especially the Trondheim area versus West Norway). The consequences were political conflicts and bloody feuds that caused great harm and destruction throughout the country.

After about thirty years there seemed to be a possibility of reestablishing order and peace. The leaders of the landed aristocracy joined hands with the bishops, headed by the Archbishop. They agreed on a new order of succession, limiting the heredity to sons born in marriage and giving the eldest son the first right. This was a great victory for the Church, which now won a privileged and powerful position in Norwegian society, in accordance with the Gregorian ideas then in vogue in Western Europe.

By this time the throne was vacant, as there was no legal pretender. Therefore a young nobleman, whose mother was a daughter of King Sigurd the Crusader, was elected king and crowned by the Archbishop. This was the first coronation in Scandinavian history. Things now looked fairly well; the new king was supported by the leading men in the country and was on the whole well liked. A new pretender, who was joined by a group of men called the *birchlegs*,[1]) was after some years defeated and killed. A small remnant of the birchlegs fled to Sweden, where by chance they met with a man who became their leader, marched together with them into Norway, and after some years of hard fighting overthrew the seemingly well established monarchy and himself became King of Norway. His name was *Sverre Sigurdson*.

In Sverre we meet one of the most outstanding, but also one of the most controversial figures in Norwegian history. There is no doubt about his political and strategical genius and, on the whole, no doubt about his intellectual ability, but great doubt surrounds his character. Was he sincere in claiming to be of royal birth and thus entitled to the throne by virtue of hereditary right, or was he only moved by ambition? And next: was he *really* the son of a king? The problem remains unsolved and is perhaps insoluble.

His work as a king was at once reactionary and progressive.

---

[1]) A nickname invented by their enemies to depict them as poor rabble. In fact many of them were poor people who for long periods stayed in the forests, and when their trousers became worn and torn they tied pieces of birch bark round their legs.

He reestablished the traditional hereditary monarchy and the supremacy of the king over the Church[1]), but on the other hand he effected considerable reforms in the local administration and the judicial system. His policy roused violent opposition under the leadership of the bishops, who founded the *bagler* party[2]) whose leader was *Bishop Nicholas* of Oslo. Against them stood the birchlegs. They now formed a respectable party, under the leadership of some of the prominent men in the country whom Sverre had raised to power and high offices . The conflict developed into a regular civil war, which lasted also after Sverre's death (in 1202). At last an armistice was arranged, and for a time the country was in fact divided into a bagler and a birchleg kingdom.

Lasting peace was restored to the country by *Haakon Haakonson* (Haakon IV) who was a grandson of Sverre. He was only 13 years old when he was proclaimed king by his adherents, and six years later he was formally accepted (1223). During the first ten years of his reign there were, indeed, some risings against him by various pretenders, but they were all put down by the brilliant *Earl Skule* (*Baardson*), who was Haakon's chief adviser and the real ruler of the country during these first difficult years. Skule was an ambitious man and had even claimed the throne, which he rightly thought himself entitled to, but his claim had been rejected in favour of Haakon. To satisfy him King Haakon gave Skule the control of one third of the kingdom and honoured him by marrying his daughter who thus became Queen of Norway. Some years later, however, Haakon deprived Skule of his political power, but permitted him to keep a large part of the royal revenues and raised him to the rank of *duke*, a title till then unknown in Norway. But Skule wanted power and still aspired to the throne, which he thought himself more qualified for than Haakon. At last he rose in open rebellion,

---

[1]) Although Sverre himself had been brought up in the house of a bishop in the Faroe Islands and had received clerical education.

[2]) From Old Norse *bagall* = crozier or bishop's staff.

but after a brief period of fighting he was defeated and killed near Trondheim in 1240. This event put an end to the civil war period[1]).

4. *Medieval Norway at its Height.*

Under Haakon IV the territorial extension of Norwegian domination reached its height. Norway proper also comprised three districts that to-day are Swedish: *Baahuslen, Jemtland* and *Herjedalen.* On the other hand *Finnmark* was as yet no part of the kingdom, but a dependency, inhabited by *Lapps,* whom both the King of Norway and the Grand Prince of Novgorod (in Russia) had a right to tax. Norway also included the western islands previously annexed, and Haakon added *Iceland* and *Greenland* by peaceful agreement. Both these countries needed imported foodstuffs, and in the treaty the Norwegian king bound himself to keep up regular supplies in return for the right of taxation.

Haakon kept a strong and well equipped navy, but he did not use it till the close of his reign. He then undertook an expedition to the Hebrides to protect them against aggression on the part of the Scottish king. The expedition was unsuccessful and on the home voyage he died in the Orkneys.

Norway had now become a member of the European family of states. This appeared in the fact that diplomatic relations were established with the most prominent states, and treaties of commerce and friendship concluded with many of them, above all with England. For the trade with England was from of old the most important for Norway. But it is significant that now the North German cities began to obtain a prominent place in Norwegian trade. The starting point of this development

[1]) The conflict between Haakon and Skule is the subject of Ibsen's drama *The Pretenders.* The characters of Haakon and Skule here are pure fiction.

was the treaty of commerce which Haakon IV made with *Lübeck* in 1250.

Under Haakon IV the administration of the country became better organised. At the royal court were gathered the leading government officials. Most important of them was the *Chancellor*, who was the head of the royal secretariat. Among his duties was to take care of the correspondence with foreign countries, and as Latin was the international language of that time, the chancellor was regularly a clergyman. For consultation the king often called prominent men of the aristocracy, and this led to the formation of a standing committee or cabinet called the *Council of the Realm*, whose function was more explicitly defined under Haakon's son and successor. *Bergen* was now the residential city of the king. Here Haakon built a palace, *Haakon's Hall*, which still exists in a restored state, having been heavily damaged several times, most recently during the Second World War. In Bergen Haakon was crowned by a papal legate, *Cardinal William of Sabina*. In his speech the Cardinal expressed his surprise at the great numbers of ships and foreign traders he saw, and he praised the high level of civilisation which the people seemed to have attained.

Haakon was very friendly to the Church and showed his good will by bestowing large gifts on her. But he refused her claims for independence. However, in accordance with the wishes of the clergy he gave his consent to a new law concerning the order of succession. The civil wars had shown the disastrous consequences of the old order and the Church for reasons of Christian ethics naturally stood for the preferential right of princes born in marriage. The new law provided that there should be only one king at a time and that the eldest legitimate son of a king was to inherit the throne unless he was doomed absolutely unfit to rule.

In a *constitution* passed under Haakon's son, *Magnus the Lawmender*, (1263—80) definite rules for the order of succession were established, and it was provided that, if there was no legal heir, the nobility and the clergy should have the right to elect a

40

new king. The constitution also established detailed rules for the administration of the country. These, indeed, gave very great power to the king, but at the same time stated that the king had to exercise his power with the advice of "his wise and good men" i.e. the Council of the Realm. The Council, which was composed of the foremost noblemen, the bishops and the royal officials, from now on became a regular political institution. On matters of the highest importance the king was supposed to summon an assembly consisting of all the noblemen and the bishops, a *parliament*.[1])

It was the great landowners who formed the nobility. King Magnus reorganised them in accordance with the social system in Europe and gave them new titles: *barons, knights* and *squires.* The barons had the duty of performing military service with a retinue of men on horseback in full equipment. In return they received certain privileges, the most important of which were exemption from taxation and the right of collecting for themselves part of the royal revenues in their several districts (*fiefs*). They soon achieved the position of *vassals* in the general European sense.

Next to the nobility ranked the high clergy i.e. the bishops, who to a great extent were recruited from among the noble families. After the establishment of the archbishopric of Nidaros, the Church had been given the same privileges as it enjoyed in other European countries, the right of electing its bishops and of having its own clerical courts. King Sverre had deprived the Church of these privileges. Now King Magnus made an agreement with the Archbishop by which he not only granted these privileges, but also added an extensive exemption from taxation. With the political position the bishops had already won as members of the Council, it may safely be said that the Church was now a partly independent power standing beside and cooperating with

[1]) This institution played an important part during the remainder of the 13th century, but later on disappeared as the power of the king increased.

the king. This position it preserved until the end of the Middle Ages, when through the Reformation it was absorbed by the State.

Magnus's greatest achievement as a legislator was perhaps the introduction of a new code of common law for the whole country instead of the existing four legal codes. In this respect Norway was ahead of all other European countries. The most important innovation in the legal code is that it made the prosecution and punishment of criminals a *public* concern. Crime was looked upon as a violation of society. But at the same time the provisions of the criminal law were based on considerations of humanity in accordance with a development that had taken place in practice during the preceding generation.

Magnus, who justly bears his surname, showed his humane and peace-loving character also in foreign affairs. Thus by peaceful agreement he ceded the Hebrides and the Isle of Man to the Scottish king, in return for a yearly tribute, which, however, soon fell into oblivion. This was, in fact, the first step towards a reduction of the Norwegian empire. The next followed two hundred years later.

Magnus was succeeded by his two sons. The younger of them, *Haakon V*, was a strong and resolute ruler. He did not call any parliament, and even in the choice of councillors he made himself more independent by abolishing the title of baron, for the barons were members of the Council by privilege. Moreover he thought that the barons in some cases had abused their right to keep armed forces by acting independently, which implied a threat to the unity of the kingdom. But Haakon used his great power with moderation. In co-operation with his council he established a system of strict supervision of the administration of the local governors.

Haakon V made Oslo not only his residential city but the capital of the country and seat of the central administration. This was a natural consequence of the general economic development, which had gradually made East Norway the most important part

42

The Nidaros Cathedral in Trondheim was finished around 1300. On the high altar of this church was placed St. Olav's shrine.

of the country. To protect the capital he built the castle of *Akershus*, which was both a fortress and a royal palace. Furthermore he built the castles of *Baahus* (in the south-eastern corner of Norway) and *Vardöhus* in eastern Finnmark. The building of the latter had its background in the fact that Finnmark was becoming a Norwegian sphere of interest thanks to an increasing fur trade. Some Norwegians had settled there, and a Christian mission had started among the Lapps, supported by the King. Vardøhus was built to protect Finnmark from Russian aggression and also as a centre of the fur trade. In addition Haakon extended the smaller fortresses already existing at Tunsberg, Trondheim and Bergen. He built all these fortresses becusae the old naval defence system (the leidang) had fallen into

43

decay and a time had come when the security of the country above all depended upon the castles. He who was master of the castles was master of the country.

In his foreign policy Haakon asserted Norway's interests and prestige with great vigour. An important point in this field was now the relations with the North German trading cities of *Lübeck* and *Rostock*, which were members of the powerful Hanseatic League. Since the time of Haakon IV they had been carrying on an increasing trade with Norway, and in 1294 they had obtained a royal charter which gave them the right to carry on import and export trade in Oslo, Tunsberg and Bergen during the summer season, and they had been granted some privileges, among them exemption from certain taxes. The background of this policy was the fact that Norway could no longer supply herself with grain and so needed imported grain. The Baltic regions had a large surplus of grain and the Hanseatic cities had succeeded in getting the trade in these regions into their hands. On the other hand Norway had goods to export, furs and skins, and, above all, dried fish.

In many ways it was advantageous for Norway that the Hanseatic cities took over the Norwegian trade. They had ships of a great carrying capacity (*cogs*), and an excellent sales organisation which controlled large markets. This created increased chances for Norwegian exports, and also the import arrangement with the German cities was advantageous as long as it was limited to wholesale trade with Norwegian merchants. But the Germans soon showed a tendency to extend their trade. They wanted to remain in the Norwegian cities all the year round and also carry on retail trade. This involved a great danger, that of a German trading monopoly with all the abuses a monopoly may entail.

Haakon V took a firm attitude to these developments and managed to keep the German merchants within the limits stipulated in the charter of 1294.

But in his later years he was full of sad forebodings about the

44

future of his kingdom. He foresaw a time when foreigners would interfere with the fate of the country. His fear did not only apply to the Germans, but was also caused by the fact that he had no male heir, and his daughter was married to a Swedish prince. After Haakon's death the Norwegian throne would by the order of succession fall to their son. There was then a possibility that this grandson might be elected king of Sweden[1]), and thus a union between the two kingdoms be established. This was what really happened in 1319, the year when Haakon V died, and his grandson, *Magnus Erikson*, became king of both countries.

[1]) Sweden had an elective monarchy.

IV. UNION PERIOD. DECLINE AND FALL.
(1319—1537)

The union brought about between Norway and Sweden in 1319 was purely personal, only the king being common to the two countries. No one expected it to become lasting and, in fact, after a couple of decades it broke up. The reason was that the leading men in Norway were discontented with the arbitrary rule of the union king, who mostly stayed in Sweden and showed little consideration for the interests of Norway. At the demand of the Norwegian Council a baby son of the king was placed on the Norwegian throne, and after he had come of age he took over as ruling king under the name of *Haakon VI* (1355—80). He was the last king of an independent and separate Norway in the Middle Ages. It was not until six centuries later, in 1905, that Norway became fully independent once more, with her own king.

After the death of Haakon VI Norway entered into a union with Denmark. The origin of this union was as follows: Haakon had been married to the Danish Princess Margaret. Their son *Olav* had some years before Haakon's death been elected King of Denmark[1]) and now succeeded to the Norwegian throne. But Olav IV died as a young man after only a few years' reign. However, the Danish-Norwegian union initiated under his short rule lasted until 1814, and Norway gradually became a dependency of Denmark. To begin with the union was simply a personal one, however. Norway had its own Council, which was responsible for the administration and made its will felt with considerable vigour.

From the year 1389 Sweden was also included in the union. Thus arose a Scandinavian union, which was brought about by *Queen Margaret*, the Danish-Norwegian Queen Mother, who

[1]) Like Sweden Denmark had an elective monarchy.

46

after her son's death succeeded in having a distant German relative acknowledged as heir to the Norwegian throne and elected King of Denmark. Some years later he was also elected King of Sweden, and in the year 1397 crowned as joint king of all three countries in the Swedish city of Kalmar, hence the name of the *Kalmar union*. This union nominally existed till 1523, but there were several periods of interruption, in which Sweden temporarily seceded.

Queen Margaret was not only the originator of the Kalmar union, but its dynamic leader as long as she lived (till 1412). She was born a Danish princess, and mostly resided in Copenhagen. But it cannot be said that she attempted to give Denmark a dominating position in the union. It was seldom that she departed from the rule saying that the realms should be governed by native men, and this especially held good for Norway. What she aimed at was a united Scandinavia with the greatest power possible for the monarch.

Margaret's successors did not continue her policy. They appointed Danes and Germans feudal lords and bailiffs in Norway and Sweden, where they oppressed the peasantry with heavy rents and taxes. This in the course of time led to several risings in the two other countries, and in Sweden the risings terminated in a national revolution under the leadership of a young nobleman, *Gustav Vasa*, who founded a new dynasty in Sweden (1523).

In Norway a growing weakness is noticeable, especially after 1450, when the *Oldenburg dynasty* came to the throne and the union between Norway and Denmark was declared to be permanent. During the following decades the decline of Norwegian power became more and more evident and the lowest ebb was reached in the political catastrophe of 1536, when the newly elected king in Denmark, at the instigation of the Danish Council, declared that Norway had ceased to exist as a separate realm and was henceforward to be only a part of the kingdom of Denmark.

The causes of this sad development for Norway have been thoroughly discussed among Norwegian historians for a hundred

47

years, but it cannot be said that a satisfactory solution of the problem has yet been given. It is possible, however, to single out some outstanding historical facts which may be said to contribute to an explanation.

In the first place must be mentioned the great calamity that struck Norway in the middle of the 14th century called the *Black Death*. It has been estimated that this plague killed about half the population, which at that time amounted to nearly 350,000. Consequently large tracts of land were laid waste for several generations, which caused a serious loss of income for the great landowners, the Church and the Government. It has been maintained that the national wealth of Norway was reduced by two thirds through the Black Death. However true this may be, it goes without saying that this calamity meant a heavy blow to Norway. But the neighbouring countries were also hit by the Black Death, and probably hit even harder because of the greater density of population. On the other hand, Norway was the poorest of the three countries, less populous[1]) and less rich in soil and other natural resources than the two others. Therefore Norway was more vulnerable, and the effects of the Black Death more fatal to Norway than to Denmark and Sweden. In a Scandinavian union Norway would naturally be the weakest part, and the Black Death made it still weaker.

Still we cannot talk of a complete national collapse as yet. The effects of the Black Death appeared more indirectly, for instance in the weakened position in relation to the Hanseatic cities. They now obtained an extension of their trading privileges, above all in Bergen, where they had already established themselves as permanent traders residing in a part of the city on the quayside called the *Office*. They gathered the whole trade of West and North Norway into their hands, and more and more formed a separate society, a state within the state, obeying only their own laws and paying no taxes to the Norwegian Government. It meant a further step towards Hanseatic domination

[1]) Sweden had 500 000 and Denmark 800,000 inhabitants.

48

when in the middle of the 15th century the Hansa merchants of Oslo and Tunsberg succeeded in bringing the trade in East Norway completely under their control. From that time the Hanseatic cities of Lübeck and Rostock had, indeed, a trade monopoly in Norway which lasted for two generations. In this monopoly the Hansa had a powerful weapon, which they used not only to secure economic advantages, but also politically to bring about the union with Denmark and to uphold it. For it often appeared that the union kings, because of their financial dependence on the Hanseatic cities, were the best promoters of Hanseatic interests. They thwarted the endeavours of the Norwegian Council to help the Norwegian burghers or to favour British and Dutch competition with the Hanseatics.

But more fatal to Norway was the effect of the Black Death on the nobility of the country. Before the Black Death there were altogether 300 noble families in Norway, after it only 60 families remained. Thus the nobility as a class was weakened, but the individual noblemen became richer by inheritance or purchase. Some of them collected hundreds of farms in their hands and founded large estates. At the same time a peculiar misfortune befell many of the noble families. They died out on the male side, only daughters being born to them. According to old established tradition noble girls could only marry their equals, and because of the shortage of Norwegian young noblemen the young ladies married Swedes and Danes. These foreigners came to Norway, took over the estates of their wives and became members of the Norwegian nobility with full rights. They obtained fiefs and held high offices, and even sat as members of the Council of the Realm. Thus the Norwegian nobility became gradually mixed up with foreign, above all Danish, elements, and these foreign elements increased in number and power during the decades before and after 1500. About the year 1530 only two members of the Council were true-born Norwegians. All the main castles were in the hands of Danes.

The denationalisation of the nobility was probably the most

"The Hanseatic Quay" in Bergen.

important cause of the weak political position of Norway in relation to the other Scandinavian states at the end of the Middle Ages. For the nobility was the leading class in those days. Members of this class sat in the Council of the Realm together with the bishops and were bearers of the national will. The bishops were all Norwegians, and the Archbishop was chairman of the Council. But they were not strong enough to oppose the foreign or half-foreign members when the foreigners took the Danish side, as they mostly did.

In this situation it appeared how disastrous it was that the Norwegian farmers, though still free men, had since the middle of the 13th century been deprived of any practical share in the political affairs of the country. Moreover Norway lacked the existence of a class of national city burghers, which in other European countries made their influence felt more and more in this period. This was a consequence, the most serious consequence, of the Hanseatic trade monopoly in Norway.

50

The lack of unity and national solidarity in the top leadership proved fatal to Norway in the course of events after 1530. These events were closely tied up with the Lutheran reformation. In Denmark Luther had won many adherents, especially among the nobility and the burghers. When the throne became vacant (1533) there were three candidates to the throne, and one of them, Prince Christian, was an ardent Lutheran. After three years of civil war his party was victorious and he was elected king under the name of *Christian III.*

In Norway the Lutheran reformation had practically no supporters apart from some of the immigrant Danish noblemen and the Hanseatic merchants in Bergen. The natural leader in the struggle for the Roman Catholic Church and against the victorious party in Denmark was the Archbishop of Nidaros, *Olav Engelbriktson.* He was a Norwegian by birth, and his struggle became at once a religious and a national fight. He fought, indeed, for a Roman Catholic and an independent Norway.

Archbishop Olav lacked neither the will nor the courage to do his utmost for Norway, but his plans were counteracted by the powerful Danes in the Council and only met with a limited support from the Norwegian people. Above all he lacked military strength. He made vain attempts to conquer the castles of *Akershus* and *Bergenhus.* His plan was to reestablish an independent Norwegian kingdom under a Roman Catholic king (his candidate was a German prince, who was supported by the Emperor Charles V). He now saw that it was necessary to give up that plan. Then, as a last resort, he tried to effect a compromise that would secure Norwegian independence under a new union king. But he did not succeed. For just then Copenhagen opened its gates to Christian III, whose victory was complete.

The Archbishop understood that his cause was lost. In the spring of 1537 he sailed away from Norway, succeeded in escaping from his pursuers and came to the Netherlands, where he died soon afterwards. Then the Lutheran reformation was forced upon Norway.

V. FROM DEPENDENCE TO NEW FREEDOM
(1537—1814)

1. *Under the Danish Nobility* (1537—1660).

The paragraph in the royal charter of 1536 which declared Norway to be no longer a separate realm but only a part of Denmark marked the lowest level in the history of the Norwegian people so far. But fortunately this paragraph was not put into effect to the letter. Norway continued to be *called* a realm, an evidence of which is the term "the twin realms" or "the dual monarchy" used in the following centuries about Norway and Denmark. The idea of the kingdom of Norway remained alive, and an idea is a psychological reality, which in the course of time may change into a material fact. That is exactly what happened in Norway, but it took nearly 300 years.

Politically, however, Norway was now *under* Denmark. It was a Danish dependency. The outward sign of this new status was the abolition of the Norwegian Council. Norway was ruled by the Danish Council, in which the *nobility* bore sway. There were no clerical members any longer. On the whole the following period of nearly 150 years was a heyday for the Danish nobility economically and politically. The establishment of the Lutheran Church had brought much of the Church lands in Denmark into their hands, and the main fiefs in Norway were practically all given to Danes in this period. Many of the minor fiefs were even awarded without any obligation for the holders to settle in the country.

In spite of these sad political facts the period is marked by progress for Norway in many ways. The most striking feature is the growth of the nation's economic strength. The material

52

effects of the Black Death were in all essentials overcome by the beginning of this period, and the great geographical discoveries about the year 1500, which made Western Europe the centre of world trade, gave new chances to Norwegian exports and shipping. By a lucky coincidence these economic activities were just then becoming Norwegian enterprises again. The beginning was made in 1508, when the first blow was aimed at the Hanseatic trade monopoly. The German merchants in Oslo and Tunsberg were in that year deprived of their privileges, and new rights were awarded to Norwegian traders in all cities. But the main stronghold of the Hanseatics, the "Office" and the "Quay" in Bergen remained untouched for another 50 years. Then also this stronghold fell, the Germans being forced to accept Norwegian law as binding for them and to compete with Norwegian traders on equal terms. Several Norwegians even settled in the "Office" which thus gradually lost its purely German character, although it continued to exist for another 200 years. Some of the German merchants did, indeed, leave Norway. But most of them remained, and new immigrants arrived, not only from Germany, but also from Denmark, the Netherlands and Scotland. But now all of them had to become Norwegian citizens. They were soon merged in the new class of city burghers that was in the making, and brought with them a good store of capital and valuable business experience.

As a consequence of the rise of a national class of businessmen, shipbuilding was started anew in Norway, and now based on up-to-date methods. It was in the Netherlands that Norwegian sailors became acquainted with shipbuilding techniques. Many of them not only served in Dutch vessels, but also took work in Dutch shipbuilding yards. In the course of the 16th and 17th centuries several shipbuilding yards were erected on the south coast of Norway, which in those days had a lively intercourse with the Netherlands, caused by the fish trade and the timber traffic. At first they built warships, later on also trading ships. Still, however, most of the exports from Norway were carried in foreign ships, German, Dutch and English. But a Norwegian merchant marine was in the making.

Among the export industries fishing still held the foremost place. But it was now largely expanded. To the old established cod fisheries of Northern Norway were now added important herring fisheries of Southern Norway. They took place on various parts of the coast, but were more and more centered on the west coast. Part of the catches was sold inland in a fresh state, but the greater part was dried or salted for export. Bergen continued to be the main centre of the fish trade. To this city the fishermen in North and West Norway carried their catches, and from here the fish was sent to the Netherlands, Portugal, Spain and Italy. Thus the Bergen merchants, who in fact had a monopoly of this fish trade, in the course of time acquired great wealth and became an economically powerful group. The poor fishermen grew completely dependent on them not only for the prices of their fish, but also for loans to procure boats and equipment.

From of old middle, eastern, and southernmost Norway had been richly supplied with forests, which had yielded timber for house- and shipbuilding and wood for fuel. But there had been little or no export of timber, and therefore the forests had been of rather small value to the owners. During the 16th century a great change took place partly as a result of the introduction of the *water-saw* about the year 1500. A few decades later, it was commonly used all over the country and gradually revolutionised the lumber trade of Norway. By means of the water-saw the timber logs could be cut into *planks* or *deals*, and it was exactly this form of lumber that was in great demand abroad, above all in the Netherlands and Scotland, later on also in England. These countries had very few forests and needed timber for the building of ships, dams and houses and also for pit-props in the mining industry.

This gave rise to the development of *saw-milling*. The next few centuries saw the growth of saw-milling on a wide scale, both of big mills producing for export and small mills satisfying only local needs. The former group of mills demanded capital, and therefore naturally fell into the hands of the city burghers, whereas the latter were run by the farmers. For the city burghers the saw-mills became one of their great sources of wealth, and many of them acquired forest lands in order to be able to acquire timber more freely. Saw-mills for the export trade were built in Oslo and also along the coast, generally at the mouths of rivers, where there gradually grew up several ports of loading, which in the course of time developed into cities. An obvious advantage was that the lumber industry provided work, full-time and part-time, for a great number of people in the country-side as well as in the cities.

Another important factor in the economic development of the country was the rise of the *mining industry*. At the beginning of modern times there was in Europe a widespread interest in the discovery of minerals, especially precious metals. In the dual monarchy, this interest naturally centred in the mountains of Norway, and it was generally believed that they must contain large hidden treasures. Thus mining was started, first at the instigation of *King Christian III*. Later on a great number of Danes flocked to the country, many of them inspired by dreams of acquiring quick wealth. From the beginning many German miners were employed, a fact which has influenced mining terminology in Norway to this very day.

The results were, on the whole, rather disappointing, but a belief in the possibilities of the mining projects stimulated the Danish administration to take a greater interest in Norway. This became evident during the reign of *King Christian IV* (1588—1648), who took a more active interest in Norway than any other of the Danish-Norwegian kings. He paid frequent visits to Norway, even to the northernmost parts of the country, and he sent out an expedition to Greenland and thus renewed the contact with this remote part of the old Norwegian empire. His name is in a special way associated with the capital of Norway.

After a fire in 1624 which completely destroyed Oslo, he ordered the inhabitants to rebuild the city farther west, behind the ramparts of the castle of Akershus, so as to be better protected. The King took an active part in the planning of the city as well as in the restoration of the castle, which had been partly destroyed by fire a hundred years earlier. To honour the city he gave it the name of *Christiania*, a name it kept till the year 1924, when the Norwegian Parliament decided to restore the old historical name.

It was during the reign of Christian IV that mining developed into an important industry. It comprised silver mines at *Kongsberg* (west of Oslo) and copper mines at *Røros* and other places in the Dovre area. From the time of Christian IV onwards, rion mines and works grew up in eastern and southernmost Norway, as far west as the city of *Kristiansand*, which was founded by Christian IV in 1641. The iron works produced iron bars and also cast-iron ware such as stoves. Apart from the silver works at Kongsberg, which were Government property, the mining industry was run by city burghers, and, together with the fish trade, shipping and the lumber industry, it formed the economic basis of the burgher class, which increased in number and wealth during this and the following period. The burgher class was partly of foreign origin, but in the course of time it became firmly rooted in the country and it became Norwegian in feeling and thinking. Indeed it was people of this class who towards the end of the period criticised the Danish administration and set forth national Norwegian demands.

The development of trade and manufactures created new sources of revenue for the state, and so the Government encouraged export industries and supported them, in accordance with the mercantile principles that were gaining the upper hand in the economic policy of the time. An alliance was formed between the King and the city burghers, in Norway as well as in Denmark, and this finally led to the establishment of an absolute monarchy in the year 1660.

56

This important constitutional change also had a background in the foreign policy of the time and the wars this led to. Thr dissolution of the Kalmar union had made Sweden independenn but it was blocked up, practically barred out from the westest sea by Norwegian and Danish provinces. To a country that we, rich in natural resources and steadily gaining material strength, this situation was felt to be unsatisfactory, and a desire for "natural boundaries" made itself felt. It became an aim for Swedish foreign policy to establish a better national security and to obtain a wider access to the sea, in the first instance by conquering part of south-eastern Norway. On the other hand, the Danish kings had not yet given up the hope of reestablishing the Scandinavian union. In the 1560's a war broke out and lasted for seven years (1563—70). The Swedes marched into East Norway and the Trondheim area and did not meet with much resistance on the part of the Norwegians. The farmers readily accepted Swedish domination and made peace separately, for they completely lacked national feeling and fighting spirit.

This revealed a great weakness in the union, and it was found necessary to create a central administrative organ for Norway. So after the war the office of *"stadtholder"* (governor general) for Norway was established (1572).

The war had been conducted by means of hired troops, and so was the first war under Christian IV (between 1611 and 1613). This war centred round the ownership of Finnmark. The Swedish king wanted to extend his kingdom northwards to the Arctic Ocean and began imposing taxes on people in the north. But Christian maintained that they were his subjects, and he led the war to a victorious end. Finnmark was recognised as part of Norway.

As a result of these wars and because of the increasing economic importance of Norway in the dual monarchy, steps were soon taken to reestablish a military defence system for Norway. It was resolved to establish an *army* consisting of 6000 foot and

500 horse, based on compulsory service among the tenant farmers for the foot while the freeholders and the noblemen were to provide horsemen. In the cities a *militia* of burghers was organised. At the same time the foundation was laid of a *navy* by hiring merchant vessels which were to serve in time of war and receive military equipment, in return for trading privileges in time of peace. Later on this new military system was considerably extended.

It was not long before the new Norwegian army and navy had to stand their test in wars against Sweden. This country was at that time in a period of great expansion. In the course of one hundred years (1560—1660) it conquered the Baltic provinces of *Esthonia* and *Latvia* and joined them with *Finland* (which had been part of Swedish territory since the 12th century) by seizing the Russian province of *Ingermanland*. Furthermore, as a result of participation in the Thirty Years' War, Sweden acquired large territories in North Germany, at the estuaries of the main German rivers (the Elbe, the Weser and the Vistula). Last but not least came the establishment of the "natural boundaries" in the Scandinavian peninsula. In the course of three wars in the 1640's and 50's Sweden conquered the Norwegian provinces of *Baahuslen, Jemtland* and *Herjedalen* and the Danish provinces of *Halland, Scania* and *Blekinge*, as well as the Danish islands of *Ösel* and *Gotland* in the Baltic.

These changes involved a complete revolution in the balance of power in the Scandinavian area. Sweden had now become the dominating state and, indeed, a great power of European dimensions.

Since the peace that ended these wars, in 1660, the boundary between Norway and Sweden has remained stable apart from a minor rectification of the border in Finnmark, which was arranged peacefully in 1751. Also the boundary between Denmark and Sweden became permanent. The attempts at reconquering the lost Danish and Norwegian provinces, which were made in he 1670's, and later in the beginning of the 18th century (the "Great Northern War", 1700—1720) led to no results. On the other hand the heavy Swedish losses of territory in Germany and the Baltic provinces in the latter war to some extent reestablished the balance of power in Scandinavia.

2. *Under an Absolute Monarch* (1660—1814).

As a result of the military defeat, the losses of territory and the heavy public debt caused by the wars with Sweden, the Danish nobility lost its political power in the dual monarchy and the king was given *hereditary* and *absolute* power. It was with the assistance of the burghers and the clergy in Denmark that this reform was effected, a reform which was, as we have seen already, prepared by earlier developments and in accordance with the general European tendencies of the time. In Norway a meeting of the Estates of the Realm (nobility, clergy, burghers and farmers) gave its consent without any opposition.

Absolutism, indeed, meant the end of all popular representation in national affairs and so, from a modern democratic point of view, it was a lamentable step. But historically seen it was advantageous, inasmuch as it did away with the oppressive domination of the nobility, whose organ had been the Council of the Realm, which was now abolished. The two countries were from now on to be ruled by the king assisted by government officials and a royal *Cabinet of Advisers*. Local affairs were also to be taken care of by officers appointed by the king. Absolutism, in fact, meant bureaucratic rule. In the new administration noblemen and people of the burgher class had equal chances and in the course of time the latter came to form the majority of the officials. The interests of the burgher class were therefore now taken better care of than before, and on the whole decisions were to a larger extent guided by considerations of the general welfare of the people.

Even from the time of the Middle Ages there had been a tendency towards concentrating commerce and handicrafts in the cities. Under absolutism this was made a guiding principle and carried out more rigidly than before. In 1662 a royal charter granted common trading rights to all cities and special privileges to each one of them. These meant that each city obtained a trade monopoly within a certain district. At the same time handicrafts were organised in local *guilds*, whose members were awarded the sole right of exercising their several crafts.

All this was in accordance with the doctrine of the mercantile system, which stood for government regulation of trade. In accordance with this doctrine, saw-milling was also regulated by law, partly with a view to *preserving* the forests, which seemed, indeed, to stand in great danger of being destroyed. By royal ordinance the number of export saw-mills was limited and so was also the yearly quantity of planks which the mills were allowed to cut. Protective tariffs and monopolies were also features of the mercantile system. Thus the iron works and glass works of Norway were given a monopoly of the Danish imports for their products, while on the other hand Denmark had a monopoly of grain imports to Southern Norway. The Finnmark trade was a monopoly first of the merchants of Bergen, then of a company in Copenhagen and at last of the Government.

From a national Norwegian point of view, the new constitution no doubt implied an advantage. Norway was no longer under the control of the Danish Council, but placed on an equal footing with Denmark under the common king. This did not mean, however, that Norway obtained a more independent position than before. On the contrary, it was the idea of the absolute monarchy to fuse the two countries into one whole. Therefore the offices of the state were open to Norwegians as well as Danes in both countries. When the two countries were separated in 1814, there were 156 Danish-born officials in Norway, and 208 Norwegian-born in Denmark. However, it should be added that in the highest offices there were practically only Danes.

Of indirect advantage to Norway was the fact that the territorial losses had made the two realms more equal in population. In 1665 Norway had about 450,000 and Denmark about 550,000 inhabitants (the Duchies of Schleswig and Holstein not included). And during the next century Norway progressed more rapidly than Denmark in population and wealth. Norway was steadily growing a more and more important part of the dual monarchy, and so it became necessary to give greater consideration to Norwegian interests.

Throughout this period, especially from 1740 onwards, there was a marked progress in the various Norwegian industries. *Agriculture* expanded through the extension of old farms and the establishment of new farms. At the same time a very important change took place in the farming class. The group of *tenant* farmers gradually dwindled, and the majority of the farmers became *freeholders*. In the middle of the 17th century only 25 % of the farmers were freeholders, whereas around the year 1800 the figure was 75 %. In the course of the 19th century tenancy completely disappeared.

The transition from tenancy to freeholdings started soon after 1660, when the government began selling thousands of the farms it possessed ("crown lands"). The reason was that the state sorely needed money to pay the public debt it had incurred through the recent wars. Another sale took place after the Great Northern War, when the state again was in need of money.

Besides the tenants several city burghers also bought crown land. Some kept it and developed estates which they ran in an excellent way, copying the implements and methods used in England and Holland. But most of the burghers sooner or later sold their land to farmers, finding it more profitable to invest money in activities other than farming.

The freeholders, in particular the bigger landowners, needed workers and obtained these through the rise of a new, subordinate class of farming men, the *cottars*. These were small-holders, who rented a house, in most cases combined with some few acres of land, from the farmer. They paid a rent and moreover had to work at the farm in summertime when needed. For this work the cottars received board and in addition a small wage. The out-

61

put of the cottars' holdings was their own property. Generally the cottars lived in poor conditions, but their position was legally secure, and they too were free men. After the great extension of cultivated land and the disappearance of tenancy, the class of cottars steadily increased from 12,000 around the year 1720 to 48,000 a hundred years later and about 81,000 in the middle of the 19th century.

A noteworthy aspect of the economic development of Norway in this period was the growth of the Norwegian *merchant marine*. It started in earnest in the latter half of the 17th century. After a temporary set-back due to the losses in the Great Northern War, the growth continued. By the middle of the 18th century Norway had nearly 600 ships, many of them rather large. In the course of the next half-century the tonnage was more than doubled. In 1807 the fleet numbered 1514 ships and reached the size of 150,000 reg.tons. It was bigger than that of Denmark and the Duchies put together, and had about 11,000 sailors. In the wars of the 18th century and the Napoleonic wars up to 1807, Denmark-Norway was neutral, and Norwegian shipping made large profits. From this time onwards Norwegian ships began plying all the seven seas. Norway had now, indeed, become a seafaring country again.

Among the old cities Bergen and Oslo had the largest mercantile fleets. Bergen was still the staple port of fish exports, while Oslo grew into a centre of lumber industry and exports. At times, however, they were surpassed by *Arendal* on the south coast and *Drammen*, west of Oslo. Each of these towns was wealthier than any Danish town apart from Copenhagen. The town population of Norway in the course of the 18th century grew from 40,000 to more than 100,000.

The economic development of the country strengthened the self-confidence and pride of the people. So did the wars against Sweden, in which the new Norwegian army and navy asserted themselves with high honour. This was particularly so in the Great Northern War, in which Denmark and Norway fought against the warlike Swedish king, *Carl XII* (Charles XII). In the last part of the war Carl made two vain attempts, in 1716 and 1718, to conquer Norway, and the "hero king" found his death in besieging the Norwegian border fortress of Fredriksten, at the town of Halden. Above all, however, the daring deeds of the naval hero, *Peter Wessel*, aroused the enthusiasm of the whole nation. He was a burgher's son of Trondheim, who had made his way up to the position of admiral of the fleet, and was at last raised to the peerage under the name of *Tordenskiold* ("thundershield").

As in the past, the exports of Norway went chiefly to Great Britain and Holland. The contact with these two countries grew more and more intimate, not only economically, but also intellectually. During the first two centuries after the Reformation, Germany had had a kind of spiritual hegemony in Norway. Now the situation changed. Well-to-do burghers often sent their sons to Great Britain to finish their education, and here they were influenced by the new, liberalising ideas that appeared in British, Dutch and French science and literature. A Norwegian-born writer of comedies and historical works, *Ludvig Holberg*, became the first spokesman of these ideas, in Denmark as well as in Norway, after spending several years of study in Great Britain, Holland, France and Italy. Gradually these ideas became integrated elements in Norwegian intellectual life.

Around the middle of the 18th century a new school of thought in economics arose in France, *physiocratism*. The physiocrats were the forerunners of the economic liberals, whose ideas were expressed by *Adam Smith* in his book, "The Wealth of Nations" (1776). They criticised the mercantile system with its trade barriers, monopolies and government regulations. *Laissez-faire* was their watch-word. "Let things take their course", they said.

During the latter half of the 18th century, these ideas had an increasing influence in Denmark and Norway, even in government circles, and the result was a considerable modification of the mercantile system. For Norway this implied the abolition of the Danish grain monopoly and the monopoly of the Finnmark trade. Furthermore, the trade and crafts regulations were modified, and the protective tariffs heavily reduced. All these changes were advantageous to Norway and greeted with satisfaction, for they gave Norwegian export trade greater chances.

The period also witnessed a flourishing of literary and scientific life. A Norwegian school of historians appeared. Snorre Sturlason's medieval masterpiece, the Chronicle of the Kings of Norway, in successive editions, had long been favourite popular reading. Even in the darkest days of national decline the Bergen pastor and historical writer *Absalon Beyer* wrote in 1567: "From the day that our country fell under Denmark and lost its own kings and masters, it has also lost its manhood strength and power, and is now growing old and grey-haired . . . But Norway may still awaken from her sleep some day, if she gets a good regent of her own."

In the latter half of the 18th century the scholarly study of Norwegian medieval history was revived. A number of books on the country's glorious past appeared to prepare the people for a resumption of national life.

The increasing prosperity among the city burghers naturally strengthened their self-confidence and fostered demands for a greater independence for Norway in economic affairs. The main demand was for an independent Norwegian *bank* to satisfy the needs of business life in Norway. This demand was voiced several times, but was always repudiated by the authorities in Copenhagen. They thought it to be contrary to their favourite idea of a Danish-Norwegian unity.

Another demand was for a Norwegian *university*. Norwegians who wanted to get an academic education in those days had to study at the University of Copenhagen (established in 1479). This particular demand bore witness to the intellectual reawakening of the Norwegian people. It was, indeed, primarily put forward by members of the bureaucracy, but warmly supported by the burgher class. These two classes were closely connected, and really formed one social group. They had the same standards of living, had social intercourse with each other, and intermarriage was frequent. The bureaucracy was to a great extent recruited from the burgher class. Nor were the farmers indifferent to the university plan, for it happened, though rather seldom, that farmers' sons studied at the University of Copenhagen.

The claim for a Norwegian university was also of long standing, but was always refused for the same reason as the claim for a bank. At last, however, after the plan had won nation-wide support and a large sum of money had been collected, permission to establish a university was granted by King Frederik VI in 1811[1]).

Thus there were in Norway several causes of discontent with the Danish administration, and among the burghers there was much criticism. In certain circles of business men in East Norway the idea of separating Norway from Denmark and uniting it with Sweden was voiced. The leading man among them was *Count Herman Wedel Jarlsberg*, a great estate owner and man of affairs and for a time a county governor, the most distinguished gentleman in the country at that time. He had been educated in Great Britain and was an admirer of the free British constitution. Absolutism he abhorred, and he was, on the basis of his experience, critical of the administration in Copenhagen. One of his reasons for favouring a union with Sweden was that this country had a free constitution (since 1809).

In spite of all this and of a few risings on the part of farmers against ruthless officials and rapacious merchants, it cannot be said that there was a spirit of revolt or a wish to break away from Denmark in the nation as a whole. The general feeling was rather one of loyalty. The separation from Denmark, when it came, was the result of external events that occurred after the dual monarchy had been forced out of its neutrality and into the whirlwind of the Napoleonic wars. This happened in the year 1807. Through a series of unlucky circumstances, the Danish

[1]) It was given the name of "The Royal Frederik's University". In 1939 the name was altered to "The University of Oslo".

government decided to side with Napoleon against Great Britain, and so Denmark and Norway became participants in the continental blockade, by which Napoleon hoped to crush the mistress of the seas economically.

For Norway this decision was ruinous. Its exports and shipping came to a standstill, and imports of foodstuffs ceased owing to the British blockade of the Norwegian coasts. Great distress and widespread starvation followed. In addition there were bad crops in 1808 and 1812 ("the black year"). For a time (1808—09) Norway also had war with Sweden, which was on the British side. In this war, too, the Norwegian army fought with honour and repelled the Swedish attacks on the country. At the same time Sweden also had war with Russia, which had made peace with Napoleon in 1807 and even gone over to his side. The Russians attacked Finland and in the course of the year 1808 conquered the whole country.

Since communication between Denmark and Norway was made difficult, the latter country had to manage her own affairs, in particular the provision and distribution of food supplies, for some years (1807—10). During this period a *Government Commission* was at the head of the administration. Count Wedel-Jarlsberg was a member of the Commission and had a leading hand in the work of securing food supplies. Then for a few years the blockade was in practice repealed, and by a special arrangement the trade between Great Britain and Norway again revived.

But in 1812 the blockade was renewed. This was a result of Napoleon's attack on Russia, which marked the beginning of a new coalition war against him. After his tragic defeat in Russia the coalition was widened, and the war of liberation from Napoleon's domination of Europe began. In this situation Sweden came to play a part which had the effect of making Norway a pawn in the political game of the great powers.

In 1809 the situation had become very critical for Sweden. After a revolution which placed a new king called Carl XIII on the throne, the country had made peace and had been forced to cede Finland to Russia. It was necessary to find an heir to the throne, as the new king was old and without children. At last, in 1810, the choice fell on one of Napoleon's most brilliant marshalls, *Jean Baptiste Bernadotte*, who in Sweden assumed the name of *Carl Johan* (Charles John).

The new crown prince at once became the leading man in Swedish foreign policy. His aim was to win Norway as a compensation for Finland and in this way also to secure peace on the Scandinavian peninsula. Therefore he joined the coalition powers against Napoleon and made treaties with Russia and Great Britain in 1812 and 1813, to which Austria and Prussia later gave their assent. By these treaties the signatory powers permitted Sweden to force Denmark to cede Norway, and they promised their diplomatic support if necessary. In return for this Sweden was to contribute an army corps under the command of Carl Johan for the final struggle against Napoleon.

After Napoleon had been defeated at *Leipzig* in October 1813, Carl Johan marched with his army corps against Denmark. The Danish king found it hopeless to put up any resistance. By the peace of Kiel in January 1814, he ceded Norway, with the exception of her dependencies, Iceland, Greenland, and the Faroes, to the King of Sweden.

1. *Striving for Freedom.*

Because of the critical international situation, King Frederik VI had sent his cousin Prince *Christian Frederik*, who was heir-apparent to the throne, up to Norway as stadtholder in the spring of 1813. The King's intention was to strengthen the ties between Norway and Denmark and to prevent Swedish conquest of Norway. The Prince was in many ways well fitted for such a task, intelligent, good-looking and charming in his manners. At once he won great popularity. Soon after his arrival he set about his task with great energy. In the autumn he called a meeting of eminent men to discuss the plan for a Norwegian bank. But the meeting also discussed the general economic and political situation of the country. It was the first time since 1661 that a body of prominent Norwegians had met and considered the affairs of the nation.

On January 24th the news of the Treaty of Kiel reached Norway. Although peace was welcome, the stipulations concerning Norway were received with bitterness by the people at large. In a letter to Prince Christian Frederik the King ordered him to leave Norway and return to Denmark. But the Prince refused to obey. He resolved to take the lead in a Norwegian resistance to the Treaty of Kiel. In order to ascertain the feeling of the nation he undertook a journey from the capital through East Norway up to Trondheim and back again by another route. Everywhere he heard protests against the cession of Norway to Sweden. The King, people said, was not entitled to cede Norway to a foreign country. If he wished to abdicate his Norwegian throne, he certainly had a right to do so. But in that event it was up to the Norwegian people to decide its future fate.

Thus the Prince was confirmed in his resolution. His first plan was to proclaim himself King of Norway by virtue of his hereditary right and, for a time at least, to rule with arbitrary power. Later on, in more peaceful times, he might perhaps give the country a free constitution. This part of the Prince's plan at once met with firm opposition. The idea of the sovereignty of the people had by this time been generally accepted among the educated classes, and they wanted a free constitution immediately.

After a consultation between the Prince and some prominent men in East Norway in the middle of February, it was decided that Christian Frederik should rule the country temporarily with the title of *regent*, assisted by a Cabinet of five members, each of whom was to be head of a government office. Elections for a constituent assembly were to take place during the following weeks and the assembly was to meet in April at *Eidsvoll*, some 40 miles north of the capital. Here a mansion belonging to a wealthy land and factory owner, *Carsten Anker*, who was a personal friend of the Prince, was placed at the disposal of the assembly. This mansion, *Eidsvoll Hall*, is still preserved as the Constitution Hall of Norway and is Government property. The Regent at once set about organising his administration, but he did not establish a Foreign Office, for he wanted to have the control of foreign affairs in his own hands. Later on this proved fatal to Norway.

As laid down, the elections took place in the churches on Sundays, and during the service which preceded the elections, the congregations took an oath that they would "defend Norway's independence and sacrifice life and blood for their beloved native country." By this oath the whole nation had taken a firm stand against the Treaty of Kiel.

The constituent assembly met on April 10th. It consisted of 112 members, over half of them government officials. Naturally it was these members that took the most active part in the deliberations, for they had a higher education and were well versed in state affairs. It soon appeared that there was a split in the assembly over the question of full independence for Norway or union with Sweden. One group, comprising a vast majority in the assembly, stood for the immediate establishment of an independent Norwegian state. The minority group, which numbered about 30 members, wanted to keep the door open for a *personal union* with Sweden, but based on full equality between the two realms. These members thought there would be little chance of having an independent Norway acknowledged by Sweden and the signatory powers. The leader of the majority group, which comprised most of the officials and farmers, was *Chr. M. Falsen*, a country judge in the Oslo region. The leader of the minority was *Count Wedel Jarlsberg*. The merchants mostly joined this group. To them peace with Great Britain was a major aim, because in their opinion it was indispensable to economic recovery.

The main task of the assembly was to draw up a *constitution*, and on this question there was no essential disagreement in the assembly. A committee was appointed to prepare a proposal. Its chairman was Falsen, and he had the leading hand in the committee work as well as in the deliberations in the assembly. He is, therefore, justly called the "Father of the Constitution".

The constitution was discussed and passed by the assembly during the first half of May, and on the 17th a fair copy was laid on the Speaker's table and read to the members. On the same day Christian Frederik was unanimously elected King. Norway was thus reestablished as a free and independent realm and had a free constitution. Therefore the 17th of May is celebrated as the independence day of Norway.

The Eidsvoll constitution established a limited and hereditary monarchy. The king was to exercise his power through a Cabinet of ministers, who were to be appointed by him and bear responsibility for his actions. They were legally, but not politically responsible to a national assembly, which was to have

The reading of the Constitution, Eidsvoll 1814.

the sole right of appropriating money and making laws. It was given the name of *Storting*, and was to consist of only one chamber, but for legislative purposes to divide itself into two sections, the *Odelsting* and the *Lagting*. Royal Assent was necessary to all Acts passed by the Storting, but the king had only a suspensive veto.

The elections for the Storting were to take place every three years on the basis of a limited franchise. Farmers, burghers and state officials had the right to vote.

The constitution was based on the idea of the *division of power* as advocated by the French political philosopher *Montesquieu*. Therefore the Cabinet members were not allowed to take part in the deliberations of the Storting, and were not to be dependent on the Storting for being in power. They were the advisers of the king and heads of the administration. So parliamentarism was not part of the Eidsvoll system.

The constitutional development in Norway after 1814 has been based on the foundations laid at Eidsvoll in that year. The constitution of present day Norway is, indeed, only a modification of the Eidsvoll constitution.

2. *Defending Freedom.*

The Eidsvoll men had finished their work. Now it remained to be seen whether the construction they had built could stand. This did not depend on Norway alone, but also on the will of Sweden and the signatory powers.

It was a lucky thing for Norway that Carl Johan had been forced to stay away from his country for several months after the peace of Kiel, as he was engaged in the final struggle against Napoleon. Not till the end of May did he return to Sweden. In the meantime it had been left to the Swedish government to take possession of Norway. But the government was rather inactive. It contented itself with issuing proclamations and sending letters, but dared not start an attack on Norway as long as the Crown Prince was away with the best regiments of the Swedish army. In this situation Christian Frederik proved a very clever diplomat. His tactics were to protract deliberations, postpone decisions, and gain time. So far he had been successful. But after Carl Johan's return the situation changed. A decision was approaching. The signatory powers sent delegates to Scandinavia to inquire into the matter. They went first to Copenhagen, and then to Oslo, where they arrived at the end of June. They soon discovered that the Norwegian resistance to the Treaty of Kiel really was in accordance with the will of the people, and not an intrigue of the Prince, as they had heard.

It was, above all, from Great Britain that Norway might hope for goodwill. In the treaty of alliance between Great Britain and Sweden of the preceding year, it was stated that the union between Norway and Sweden ought to be brought about peacefully, and that the greatest possible consideration should be given to the happiness and liberty of the Norwegian people. Placing his trust in this, Christian Frederik had in March sent Carsten Anker to London to try to obtain support for the cause of Norway. He was met with sympathy by some Members of

Parliament, but the Government declared that the promise to Sweden had to be kept. However, it was in the interest of Great Britain to secure for Norway as large a degree of independence as was compatible with the union. It did not want to have an amalgamation of the two countries, which would make Sweden overpowerful among the Scandinavian countries and thereby give its allies Russia and Prussia too strong an influence in this region. This viewpoint was shared by Austria.

There were, in fact, certain chances for Norway, at least to preserve its constitution. But one thing soon became clear. King Christian Frederik had to abdicate the throne. On this point the powers were unanimous. The King himself understood that this was necessary. But he informed the delegates that he was bound by the constitution and must leave the decision to the Storting. The delegates accepted this, and declared themselves willing to negotiate an armistice between Sweden and Norway. The negotiations led to an agreement on all points but one. The demand for Swedish occupation of two fortresses in south-eastern Norway near the Swedish border was refused. Therefore war broke out at the end of July.

The war lasted for only a fortnight. The plan of the Swedes was, as in past wars, to aim a decisive blow at the capital through south-eastern Norway. Their forces were far superior to the Norwegians in number, equipment and military training, and they stood under the command of one of the most eminent generals of the time. In spite of their inferior numbers the Norwegians were successful where real fighting took place. On the northern wing of the front, near the little town of Kongsvinger, a detachment won repeated victories over a Swedish regiment and drove it across the border. But on the main part of the front, farther south, the Norwegian army, by order of the King, retreated without risking a real battle.

3. *Effecting a Compromise.*

There were good chances that the campaign would end in a Swedish victory, but this might take a much longer time than Carl Johan had calculated. For various reasons he was anxious to have the Norwegian affair settled before the Congress of Vienna was due to meet. He knew that he, an upstart of the French revolution, was not exactly popular among the legitimate dynasties that were now masters of Europe again.

Therefore Carl Johan was willing to accept an armistice and a political compromise. An agreement was concluded on August 14th stating that an extraordinary Storting was to be called for the beginning of October, and negotiations for a union were to take place between the Storting and Swedish commissioners. Carl Johan promised to accept the Eidsvoll constitution, with only such amendments as were necessary consequences of the union. Christian Frederik on his part promised to abdicate the throne as soon as the Storting had met, but in a secret article bound himself to retire at once under pretext of illness and to leave the rule of the country to the Cabinet.

The Norwegian view was that this agreement implied two very important advantages. The Eidsvoll constitution had been saved, and the union would be based on the will of the Norwegian people, not on the Treaty of Kiel.

The Storting met at the appointed time. It soon became evident that the union was unavoidable. The Storting therefore resolved, almost unanimously, that on certain conditions Norway should be united with Sweden under one king. But it refused to elect the king before the conditions had been agreed upon. After an agreement had been reached, the Swedish King Carl XIII was unanimously elected King of Norway.

In the next year a union contract was drawn up to define the scope of the union, and was passed by the Storting and the Swedish Diet ("Riksdag"). It stated that the two realms were to have one king and stand together in war, but in all other respects be independent of each other and on an equal footing. From the very start, however, Norway in fact had an inferior position. An important feature was the lack of a Foreign Office and a Foreign Service for Norway, for Christian Frederik had, as before mentioned, omitted to establish a Foreign Office, (see page 69). Now the Foreign Minister, the ambassadors and the consuls of Sweden were acknowledged as functioning also for Norway. Another mark of inferiority was a new paragraph in the constitution, which authorised the king to appoint a stadtholder in Norway. But nothing of this was mentioned in the union contract.

During the first few years of the union Norway had no flag of her own. But in 1821 she got her own merchant flag (like the present flag), which, however, could not be used south of Cape Finisterre in Spain. Here Norwegian ships had to fly the Swedish flag. The background of this was that the pirate state of *Algeria* had an agreement with Sweden by which it promised to respect the Swedish flag. The naval flag was like the Swedish, only with a union symbol in the left hand top corner.

As the king mostly lived in Sweden, it was necessary for a section of the Norwegian Cabinet to stay in Stockholm to act as advisers to the king in Norwegian affairs. In some cases joint meetings of the Norwegian and Swedish Cabinets could take place to settle affairs of common interest to both countries. But foreign affairs were not among them. For according to the Swedish constitution, foreign affairs were in the hands of the king, advised only by the Foreign Minister and another member of the Swedish Cabinet.

VII. NORWAY IN UNION WITH SWEDEN
(1815—1905)

1. *Depression and Recovery. Defence of the Constitution.*

It was under rather difficult circumstances that the reborn Norwegian state began its existence. The preceding seven years had told heavily on the nation, and the economic crisis that followed the Napoleonic wars also hit Norway. It was above all the export industries and shipping that felt the effects of the depression. Thus the lumber trade met with serious obstacles in its biggest market, Great Britain, which imposed a high duty on Norwegian timber in order to support the Canadian lumber industry. The iron and glass works had similar difficulties. They had till then had an open market in Denmark, but after the separation they had to pay high import duties there. These industries were concentrated in East Norway and the Trondheim area, and many people here, in the towns as well as in the countryside, suffered greatly from the depression. Many of the leading business firms went bankrupt. There was a great shortage of money. Loans were only to be had at high interest, in many cases 20 % and more. The depression period lasted for a few decades. In the course of the latter half of the 1830's things righted themselves.

In West Norway the fishing industry met with difficulties for a while because of competition with Newfoundland fish in the European markets. But this did not last very long. After a few years, Norwegian fish recaptured its old European markets without superseding the Newfoundland fish, for both were now needed, and before long fish exports were doubled in quantity. And so the fisheries flourished again.

By far the biggest industry in Norway was agriculture, which occupied 80 % of the population. Farming was still mainly based on self-supply. Money economy had not begun to dominate rural life as yet. Consequently the farmers as such felt practically no bad effects from the depression. Good crops for them meant more than high prices, and fortunately the crops were fairly good in most of those years. Another matter is that the farmers who were also forest owners suffered from the depression. But in spite of all, it may be said that the depression had a limited impact in Norway.

However, there was another factor that created difficulties of various kinds for the whole nation, the currency system, which was in great disorder. A large mass of bank-notes were circulating, partly carried over from the Danish period, partly issued by authority of the Eidsvoll assembly. These notes were constantly sinking in value, and this resulted in a steady rise in prices.

To create a stable currency the Storting in 1816 resolved to establish a *Bank of Norway*, authorised to issue bank-notes, which were to be redeemable in silver, the *silver dollar* ("speciedaler"). It was therefore necessary for the Bank to have a silver fund, and this was to be procured through a special tax, payable in silver. It is a proof of the straitened circumstances in which the Norwegian people lived that the tax did not come near to yielding the necessary quantity of silver. Two years later the Storting resolved to repeal the redemption duty, and consequently the banknotes began to sink in value and prices to rise. However, in 1822, the fall was stopped and the rate of exchange stabilised for a time. But in the course of the next twenty years the rate was gradually raised, until in 1842 par value was reached and the redemption duty reintroduced. This process meant a continuous sinking of prices and caused considerable difficulties in business life. It was a hard cure, but in the long run healthy. For in this way Norway obtained a stable currency, which it preserved till the year 1914. It made no difference to the general stability of currency that in 1875 the "daler" (dollar) was replaced by the "krone" (crown) redeemable in gold[1]).

In the course of the same period the state finances were also put in order. Heavy taxation was necessary, for at the outset the Norwegian Government was short of credit. Not till 1820 did it obtain a foreign loan, and only on very hard terms. Two years later it got a new loan, which was not much better. But the state of Norway proved a punctual payer of interest and instalments, and that had the beneficial effect of creating confidence in Norway in the international money market. The terms were somewhat relieved, and new loans were obtained that were more favourable. But before long the Government ceased contracting debts. Strict economy and liquidation of the public debt became the guiding principle of the financial policy. This policy succeeded very well. By 1850 the Norwegian state was free from debt.

Besides economic and financial problems, it was the defence of the Constitution that mostly occupied the Norwegian mind in the first part of this period. The Norwegian constitution was the most democratic in Europe at that time. Carl Johan (King from 1818), although he certainly was not in favour of absolutism, found the constitution somewhat too democratic, and wanted to have more power for the King. This was partly due to the opposition his policy had often met with in the Storting. Therefore, in 1821, he brought in several bills for amendments to the constitution which aimed at increasing the royal prerogatives. When they came up for debate in 1824 they were unanimously rejected by the Storting. But Carl Johan did not give in. He continued to introduce his bills throughout his whole reign (he died in 1844). They were repeatedly rejected, in the end without even being discussed in committee. The basic principles of the Eidsvoll constitution were to remain unaltered.

One of the bills aimed at giving the King the right of dismissing state officials, with the exception of judges, without a trial.

[1]) Onewas exchadollar nged for four crowns.

The background of this amendment was that in the Storting the state officials continued to play the leading rôle as they had done at Eidsvoll. And so the irritation which the King had often felt at the opposition of the Storting to his policy was naturally directed against the state officials, although only a section of them had been among his opponents in the Storting. Another bill aimed at giving the King an absolute veto on Acts passed by the Storting. According to the constitution he had only a suspensive veto.

It was in this same year, 1824, that some people began to celebrate the 17th of May, in grateful memory of the achievements of the Eidsvoll assembly, the free constitution and national independence. King Carl Johan at first disliked these celebrations very much, because he looked upon them as demonstrations against the union and himself, and in favour of Christian Frederik, who in 1814 was elected king on that day. This was a misjudgment on his part, for in spite of his occasional conflicts with the Storting Carl Johan was highly respected and on the whole very popular in Norway. He soon understood his mistake and gave up his opposition.

From then onwards the celebration of the 17th of May became a regular festival all over Norway. This was chiefly due to the activity of the great poet *Henrik Wergeland*. He never tired of praising Norway's free constitution, on the genesis of which he wrote a book. He wanted to make it a living reality in the people's mind, not only a memory, and also to impress on them their obligation to make further progress and build on the foundations laid at Eidsvoll.

2. *Liberalism and Nationalism.*

Around the year 1830 conditions became favourable for such a development. The July revolution in France in that year created a better atmosphere for liberal and national movements than had been the case in the preceding years, the period of the Holy Alliance.

Politically liberalism in Norway took the form of a more active participation in politics on the part of the farmers. Till then they had only to a limited extent made use of the great possibilities for political power which the constitution gave them. They lacked self-confidence and elected a great number of state officials as members of the Storting. Besides they were discontented with the state of things in the new nation and felt ill-will towards the Storting, which imposed hard taxes and granted high salaries to the officials. Many of them found that they had been far better off under absolutism, and in 1818 a revolt even broke out in East Norway, instigated by a gentleman farmer in the district of Lake Mjösa. Hundreds of farmers marched towards the capital in order to abolish the Storting and give absolute power to the king. However, before they reached Oslo, they were persuaded to return home again. So nothing came of the revolt.

From the year 1830 the farmers in general began to change their attitude to the Storting. Clever agitators urged them to elect more people of their own class to the Storting and thus make the Storting an instrument for promoting their interests. The effect of this propaganda appeared in the Storting that met in 1833. Here the farmers had 45 members as against 38 officials and 17 merchants. The farmers were thus the largest group, and they had an eminent leader called *Ole Gabriel Ueland*, a small farmer and schoolmaster from south-western Norway. Their political programme advocated strict economy in the state and abolition of all extra taxes and duties yielded by the farmers. They also wanted to do away with what was still left of the town privileges. Generally speaking their main aim was to increase the political power of the people and reduce that of the state officials in all fields. Therefore a main issue was the introduction of *local self-government*.

Since the middle of the 17th century there had grown up a limited self-government in various fields, in the towns as well as in the countryside. But on the whole the local administration was still in the hands of the bureaucracy. Seen in relation to the democratic principles established in the state through the Eidsvoll constitution, this seemed illogical. Therefore the Government was also in favour of establishing local self-government by the people and introduced a public bill to that effect. After some controversy over details the bill was finally passed and received royal sanction on January 14th 1837.

From that year elected assemblies (parish councils, town councils and county councils) dealt with local affairs, under the supervision of the Government. This system aroused a new active interest in public problems among the people, and participation in local bodies became for many good training for later activity in the Storting.

Closely linked with the liberal tendencies in many countries at this time was a general national revival inspiring a struggle for freedom. In Norway there was a growing discontent with the inferior position held by Norway in the union, and claims for improvement became loud. It was demanded that Norway should have a share in foreign affairs, and a result was achieved in 1835. It was decided that henceforward the head of the Norwegian Cabinet section in Stockholm was to participate in the handling of diplomatic affairs that concerned Norway, and that the consuls were to be appointed in a joint session of the Norwegian and Swedish Cabinets and take an oath also as Norwegian officials.

Next came improvements concerning the national symbols. In 1838 Norwegian ships were permitted to use the Norwegian merchant flag on *all* seas, since, after the French conquest of Algeria in 1830, there was no reason for the limitation any longer. And finally in 1844 Norway also obtained her own *naval* flag, which was like the merchant flag, with a union symbol placed in the left hand top corner. At the same time the *Royal Seal* was designed in a way that was acceptable to Norwegian feeling. It was Carl Johan's son, *Oscar I.* who as one of his first acts granted these concessions. They were termed his "morning gift" and were received with general satisfaction in Norway.

One of the politicians who had taken an active part in the work for these improvements pointed out that, according to the union contract, Norway had a legal right to establish full equality for herself in the union by organising her own Foreign Service with a Foreign Minister as its head. But no one dared join him at that time. It was not till near the end of the century that his idea was taken up and made the programme of a political party.

Elements of nationalism also appeared in the literary and intellectual life of Norway. The outstanding spokesman of nationalism was Henrik Wergeland. He believed that the new Norway must build its cultural life on Norwegian traditions and create a literature that was coloured by Norwegian nature, Norwegian national character, and Norwegian conditions. He felt it was vital to move away from the close cultural dependence on Denmark which was a natural product of the long centuries of union. Wergeland's view did not imply a belief in intellectual isolation from the world outside. On the contrary, he was in favour of broad international contact. He sympathised warmly with the liberal movements and national struggles in other countries, and gave expression to his feelings in wonderful poems.

His nationalist views also led Wergeland to take up the language problem. From the union period Norway had taken over Danish as her official and literary language. Wergeland pleaded for a "language reform" through adopting words and phrases from the Norwegian dialects and thus gradually changing the written language. His work was continued by the editors of Norwegian folks tales and legends, *Asbjørnsen* and *Moe*. They went a step further by altering the *syntax* so as to achieve harmony with the language spoken by the people. Along these lines the reform of the Dano-Norwegian written language has been carried on to this very day and has been supplemented by changes in orthography and grammar. The background of this language reform is the fact that Danish and Norwegian are closely related languages and have much in common.

82

Another idea was to use the popular tongue as the basis of a new Norwegian written language. This idea was launched and put into practice by *Ivar Aasen*, a self-educated philologist. On the basis of the rural dialects in West Norway and the mountain regions, he wrote a grammar and compiled a dictionary of the new language. Before long a literature grew up in this language (Neo-Norwegian), which towards the end of the century was acknowledged as official along with the Dano-Norwegian language. Thus arose the bi-lingual situation that still exists in Norway.

Besides the language in past and present, the history of the country was also made the subject of careful research in the period around the middle of the century. Eminent historians wrote scholarly works on medieval Norway, and the Old Norse literature was reedited in reliable texts and commented on. Moreover the hidden literary treasures from the "dark centuries" (folk tales, legends and ballads) were re-discovered and published. All this made a strong impact on literature in the years from 1840 to 1870. It was the age of *national romenticism*.

This period also witnessed the birth of Norwegian drama. The new National Theatre in Bergen appointed a young man by the name of *Henrik Ibsen* as its director in 1851: He stayed there for a number of years and wrote several historical plays before moving to the capital.

3. *Foreign policy. Scandinavianism.*

It is a fact, paradoxical though it may seem, that simultaneously with the national-romantic revival in literature and art a strong Scandinavian movement made itself felt in the three Northern countries. This movement not only aimed at promoting peaceful friendship and brotherhood between these nations, but also advocated mutual assistance, including military aid, in case of need. The movement was mainly limited to university students and other intellectual circles and was idealistic in character. But as the Cabinets in those days consisted of intellectuals, there was a chance that the day-dreams might some day become a

83

political reality. However, it must be admitted that only a few responsible politicians in Norway and Sweden joined the movement. But the union kings of this period, Oscar I, and his son, Carl XV, were whole-hearted Scandinavianists and occasionally dreamed of uniting the three Northern countries under their sceptre.

Large Scandinavianist rallies of students were held from time to time in the university cities, at which high-flown speeches were delivered and solemn promises made. Denmark was the country which was threatened by real danger, owing to the German population in her southern provinces, the Duchies of Schleswig and Holstein[1]). The Germans here showed an increasing desire to separate from Denmark, and in the spring of 1848 a rising broke out, which was supported by Prussia. The Prussians defeated the Danish troops and threatened to invade Jutland. In this situation the King of Denmark appealed to King Oscar I for help, and the latter promised men for defending Jutland but not the Duchies.

The Storting at the end of May gave its consent to the sending of Norwegian troops to defend Denmark, but only on one condition. There should be "no further connection with Denmark". The idea of a new "Kalmar union" did not appeal to Norwegian statesmen.

A Swedish-Norwegian Army was then sent into Scania, but only Swedish soldiers crossed into Denmark, and it was only a little body of volunteers that took an active part in the 1848 campaign, among them 114 Norwegians. Meanwhile the Russian Czar, *Nicholas I*, by a direct threat had forced the Prussians to withdraw from Jutland into Schleswig. As a result of Russian and British influence negotiations began, and an armistice was finally signed on September 1st.

Next spring a new rising broke out in the Duchies, and Den-

---

[1]) Schleswig was old Danish territory, which since the 13th century had been a duchy under the Danish crown. Its southern border was the river Eider. Later on Schleswig was united with the German province of Holstein and partly germanised.

mark revoked the armistice. But King Oscar now showed little willingness to help Denmark, because he had come to share the view of his Norwegian advisers that only the northern part of Schleswig could justly be regarded as Danish territory. However, after a new Danish defeat, he consented to a peaceful occupation of Northern Schleswig by Swedish and Norwegian troops, while the terms for a reestablishment of Danish sovereignty over the Duchies were being settled by the powers.

Russia had, indeed, rendered Denmark a great service in 1848. But it was not in her interest to see Denmark as part of a united Scandinavia, which would constitute a serious menace to her northern flank. On the other hand, a curtailing of Russian territory and an expansion of Sweden-Norway would provide good chances of bringing Denmark into the union. It was this viewpoint that decided the foreign policy of King Oscar and his Swedish advisers in the 1850's. The pro-Russian policy pursued by Carl Johan was replaced by a western orientation. With the help of Great Britain and France there might be a chance of reconquering Finland in connection with the *Crimean War.*

At the outbreak of this war in 1854, King Oscar declared Sweden-Norway neutral, but at the same time he refused to close the Swedish ports in the Baltic to foreign warships, as Russia wished him to do. British and French naval forces were sent to the Baltic, and, had the western powers made this sea a main theatre of operations, it is probable that Oscar would have joined them with a view to reconquering Finland.

This policy had in part a Norwegian background. There had for years been a standing controversy over the border between Norway and Finland, in connection with Russian complaints about Norwegian reindeer pasturing on Finnish soil. Ample evidence was produced to show that the Czar had plans for annexing part of Finnmark. In spite of this, Oscar hesitated. He did not join the war, but in November 1855 he concluded a treaty with Great Britain and France by which he bound himself to cede no territory in either of his kingdoms to Russia, and in return he received an Anglo-French promise of military aid in case of Russian aggression.

The "November Treaty" was of a defensive character, but nevertheless was the subject of great displeasure in Russia, where it was regarded as a threat against the country. It remained in force till the dissolution of the union in 1905.

As the November treaty partly had a Norwegian background, it had the effect of awakening in Norway a certain interest in a united Scandinavia as a defence for North Norway against Russian aggression. This growing interest was further stimulated by the crown prince (afterwards King Carl XV) who came to Oslo as vice-roy in 1856. He took a special interest in the army, and at once appointed a committee to consider measures by which the army could be increased, improved, and above all brought under *union control*.

The tendencies towards Scandinavian unity under the Bernadotte dynasty were also stimulated in other ways. The largest of all the student meetings was held at Uppsala in 1856 and even received direct encouragement from King Oscar and King Frederik[1]) of Denmark. What was more important, however, it seemed as if Napoleon III of France would support Oscar's candidature to the Danish throne. Accordingly, next year Oscar offered a military alliance to defend Denmark and Schleswig up to the line of the river Eider. But Frederik wanted the treaty to include also Holstein, with its wholly German population, and so the date of agreement was postponed indefinitely.

That same year Oscar was taken fatally ill and died two years later. During the King's illness the crown prince reigned as regent, and after his death ascended the throne. Carl XV continued his father's Scandinavianist policy with enthusiasm. He

---

[1]) Frederik VII, who was without an heir. The chances of a Scandinavian union under the Bernadottes were closely connected with the question of the succession to the Danish throne, which was a complicated problem. Prince *Christian of Glücksburg*, a distant relative of King Frederik VII, had been conditionally nominated by the powers as candidate.

dreamed of being the liberator not only of Finland but of Poland as well. Meanwhile the Danish king had dropped his plan of preserving Holstein as part of the Danish monarchy and declared himself to be content with Schleswig. Therefore Carl in the summer of 1863 offered Frederik a military alliance promising that 20,000 Swedish and Norwegian troops should be used to defend the Eider line against a German attack. A victorious defence — and Carl believed firmly in victory — would form a good basis for his candidature to the Danish throne.

But nothing came of it. Neither the Swedish nor the Norwegian Cabinet would give their consent to an alliance unless Great Britain and France promised their support. When King Frederik died some months later, Christian of Glücksburg came to the throne without any protest. One of his first acts was the incorporation of Schleswig in the kingdom in conflict with treaty obligations, and the consequence was war with Prussia and Austria in January 1864.

In this war Denmark was left to fight alone against overwhelming forces. The Norwegian statesmen followed the lead of the Swedes in refusing to promise military support unless Great Britain or France were willing to come to the assistance of Denmark. The result of the hopeless fight was that Denmark lost both Holstein and Schleswig.

This brought bitter disillusionment to the enthusiastic Scandinavianists. The high-flown phrases had proved to be empty bubbles, which burst on the day when action was demanded. Henrik Ibsen gave expression to these feelings in several poems and in the two dramas *Brand* and *Peer Gynt*.

The year 1864 marked the end of Scandinavianism and also of national romanticism. A sober realism now made its entrance in literature as well as in politics. Ibsen drew a vivid picture of contemporary Norwegian society in powerful dramas such as *A Doll's House*, *Ghosts* and *An Enemy of the People*. In political life during the 1870's and 1880's, little interest was taken in foreign affairs, while home problems loomed large.

4. *Economic Progress. Social Changes.*

Shortly after 1814 the low tariff system which had been established in Denmark and Norway in 1797 was replaced by a system of rather high protective tariffs. About the middle of the century, in accordance with the free trade policies then in vogue in western Europe, the protective tariffs were reduced and gradually entirely abolished on foodstuffs as well as on manufactures. A beginning was made in 1842 and the end reached by 1870. From that year Norway was decidedly a free trading country till the beginning of the 20th century when she returned to a certain measure of protectionism. Liberal principles were applied also in inland trade. The craft guilds were abolished, as were the town privileges and the privileged saw-mills. The leading man in this policy was *Professor A. M. Schweigaard*, who was a member of the Storting from 1842 till his death in 1870.

These years marked a turning point in the economic history of the country. A development started which in the course of a hundred years transformed Norwegian society. It was the dawn of modern Norway, the Norway of machines in agriculture and in factories, of mechanized means of travelling and transportation, of intense business activity, of growing contact with other countries and more contact too between the various parts of the country itself.

In the old established main branch of the economy, agriculture, important changes took place. Till then production of grain had played the major part. Norway supplied three fourths of her need for grain through her own yields. All this now changed. Production of grain was greatly reduced as a result of the abolition of protection and the importation of cheap grain from America and Russia. In return farming now mainly concentrated on cattle breeding and dairy farming. Milk, butter, cheese and potatoes became the chief products. Another change was that the farmers now produced for *sale* to a much larger extent than before. Farming became much more of a business. Therefore it was necessary to make it more efficient through the use of better methods and implements. This led to a demand for professional knowledge. To meet this demand agricultural schools were established all over the country, and at the end of the century a national agricultural *college* for teaching and research work was erected in *Aas*, south of Oslo. The transition from self-supply to sales production in agriculture was made possible by the rise of manufacturing industries and the construction of railways and roads. This created markets for the farmers' products and made transportation easier.

The industrial revolution started in Oslo and Bergen with the rise of textile industries there in the 1840's. Next came paper, pulp and cellulose factories in the 60's, mainly in eastern and southernmost Norway. The latter industry developed into an important factor, based as it was on the rich forests of Norway. The biggest enterprise in this field was the *Borregaard* factories at Sarpsborg, started by a British firm, but taken over by a Norwegian company after World War I. In the 70's *fish canning* began in the city of Stavanger and in the course of time a large number of factories grew up here. Stavanger still holds the first place in this industry.

The fisheries had till then been restricted to the coasts. Now they moved out to the banks, and then open boats were replaced by deck boats. Later on steam-engines and motors took the place of oars and sails, and new fishing methods were employed. Sealcatching and whaling were carried on in the Arctic Ocean and later on, especially after 1900, also in the Antarctic. The invention of the *harpoon gun* by the Norwegian skipper *Svend Foyn* laid the technical basis for the development of whaling into an industry of international dimensions.

But above all it is the tremendous growth of the *merchant marine* that distinguishes the period. This growth was due to the colossal increase in world trade, which was a consequence of the progressing and expanding industrial revolution in Europe

89

and America. There was an ever-increasing demand for transportation, and Norwegian skippers and shipowners cleverly utilised the chances that were offered. From 1850 to 1880 the total tonnage grew from 284,000 to $1^1/_2$ million tons. This was the glorious age of the sailing-ships, which still survives in popular tradition, full of romance and poetry. The growth of the fleet continued up to World War I, when the tonnage amounted to about $3^1/_2$ million and the Norwegian merchant marine ranked as number three in the world. From the 1880's the sailing-ships were gradually replaced by steamships, and by 1920 the transition was completed. During the First World War half the tonnage was lost, torpedoed or blown up, but the fleet was restored and augmented in the inter-war period, so that at the outbreak of the Second World War Norway had a merchant marine of nearly 5 million tons, 3 million of which were motorships and 2 million tankers.

Inland communications also developed speedily. The first Norwegian railway was opened for traffic in 1854. It was owned by a private company, in which the Government had shares, and it had been constructed by an English engineer, *Robert Stephenson* (son of George Stephenson). Later on the Government took over the building and running of most railways. The most spectacular railway is the one running from Oslo to Bergen across the mountains. It was finished in 1909.

Parallel with the construction of railways went the building of macadam roads all over the country and the establishment of steamship routes along the coast and in the fjords. The latter were run by private companies, but were subsidised by the Government. In the 1850's the first telegraph wires were laid and in the 80's came the first telephone wires.

As a result of all these changes in the economic field the urban section of Norwegian society increased greatly in the course of the following hundred years. In 1850 only 12 % of the people lived in cities. Fifty years later the urban population was 28 % and one hundred years later 32.5 %. But to this last figure must be added the number of people living in suburbs and in industrial centres in the countryside, altogether 20 %. Thus the urban section of Norwegian society to-day comprises over half the population.

5. *Norwegian Emigration.*

In spite of the expansion in Norwegian industries which took place from 1850 onwards, it proved impossible to provide work for all adults. Economic expansion did not keep pace with the increase in population. The solution of this problem was found in emigration to other parts of the world, notably to North America.

In 1825 the first group of emigrants, about 50 people, sailed in a little vessel from Stavanger to the United States. Ten years later another group left, and from then "America fever" began to spread, first to West Norway and the upper valleys in the East, later on to all parts of the country. But it was not till the middle of the 1860's, after the American Civil War, that emigration assumed a comprehensive character, which lasted for half a century. From 1866 to 1915 nearly $^3/_4$ million Norwegians emigrated. There were three big waves of emigration, the biggest in the years between 1879 and 1893, in which $^1/_4$ million emigrants left Norway. In the top year 1882 no less than 30,000 Norwegians emigrated and the population of the country decreased. The 1880's were economically a hard time in Norway.

During the First World War emigration ceased, and when it started again at the beginning of the 1920's new American immigration laws limited it to a minimum, and the financial crisis of 1929 put an end to all emigration to USA.

Norwegian emigrants mainly settled in the Middle West, notably in Wisconsin, Minnesota and the Dakotas. Many also went to live in the state of Washington. Certain areas were almost wholly occupied by Norwegians, for instance the Red River Valley on the border of Minnesota and Dakota. In this century not a few Norwegians have emigrated to Canada. Altogether there are several million people of Norwegian descent in the United States and Canada.

6. The Thrane Movement.

The first labour organisation in Norway was founded in the year 1849 by *Marcus Thrane,* an academic idealist, who was influenced by the ideas of Louis Blanc and other French socialists. His organisation mainly consisted of journeymen, workers, and cottars, and in the course of a few years it obtained a membership of 20,000. Though he was avowedly a socialist himself, Thrane's actual programme was limited to practical reforms such as universal suffrage, old age pensions, abolition of the grain duties and reform of the cottar system. Unfortunately the movement caused some local riots, and in a national congress of the organisation some members imprudently hinted the possibility of armed sedition. Thrane and the other leaders firmly opposed these utterances, but in spite of this they were arrested and indicted with sedition. They were convicted and sentenced to several years' hard labour.[1]) The organisation was dissolved, and the movement died out. It was not till the industrial revolution had begun to transform Norwegian society that time was ripe for labour organisations in Norway.

In spite of its failure the Thrane movement had immediate effects on Norwegian political life by causing a split among the farmers. The great landowners had been frightened by the new radicalism, especially perhaps by the demand for a reform of the cottar system. They now began to side with the state officials and the burghers in support of the government. But the main body of farmers, under Ueland's leadership, were sympathetic to the labour programme and continued as an opposition group together with the liberal intellectuals, who represented the middle class elements in the cities. This was the prelude to the formation of the first two political parties in Norway, the Conservative and the Liberal Party.

[1]) After he had served his term, Thrane himself emigrated to USA, where he took an active part in the socialist movement.

7. *Party Politics. The Constitutional Conflict.*

According to the constitution of 1814 in its final form, the King had a right to appoint a stadtholder in Norway (p. 75). To begin with, Swedes were appointed for this office, but after 1836 only Norwegians were appointed. Still the Norwegian people felt that the office of stadtholder was humiliating to Norway, and there was a general desire to have it abolished. In accordance with this desire the Storting in 1859, against 2 votes, passed an amendment to this effect. The King (Carl XV) had beforehand promised to give his assent, and everybody regarded the abolition as a fact. But then an unexpected obstacle arose.

In Sweden the resolution of the Storting was met with a storm of protests. It was claimed that Swedish consent was necessary, as the stadtholder clause in the Norwegian constitution was alleged to be part of the agreement between the two countries in 1814. Especially in the House of Nobles[1]) threatening speeches were delivered which not only protested against the amendment, but also demanded a revision of the union contract in such a way that Sweden, as the bigger country, was secured a superior position in the union. The King at last yielded to the pressure of Swedish opinion and refused his assent. But he did so in a *Norwegian* Cabinet meeting (not a joint meeting of the two Cabinets) and thereby showed that he considered the question as a merely Norwegian concern. The Norwegian Cabinet countersigned the royal veto.[2])

This event had far-reaching consequences in Norwegian politics. In the next year the Storting unanimously passed a resolution in which it protested against the Swedish views and maintained the principle of full equality within the union and full sovereignty for either nation in all matters which were not explic-

[1]) The Swedish Diet was then still composed of four estates: nobles, clergy, burghers, and farmers.

[2]) In 1873 the problem was solved peacefully. The new King (Oscar II) gave his assent, and no Swedish protests were heard.

93

itly mentioned in the union contract. This resolution formed the basis of Norwegian policy in the union issue as long as the union lasted, namely till 1905.

The stadtholder affair also had lasting consequences because of the impression it made on a young Norwegian politician who at that time was making his way upwards and soon came to the front rank as a champion of Norwegian independence and democratic constitutional reforms.

This man was *Johan Sverdrup*, a clever lawyer, well versed in political history and constitutional law, and a brilliant orator. He had been a member of the Storting since 1851. He felt convinced that a Cabinet which was founded on the majority of the Storting and thus really representative of the Norwegian people would have resigned rather than allow a royal veto to be used at foreign command. Therefore he became an ardent advocate of *parliamentary government*.

Towards the end of the 1860's Sverdrup succeeded in uniting the intellectual liberals and the farmers in the Storting under his leadership. This was settled by an agreement between Sverdrup and *Sören Jaabæk*, a small freeholder from southernmost Norway, who was now in fact the leader of the main group of farmers in the Storting. He had also founded a nation-wide organisation of farmers and exercised great influence as a newspaper editor. Jaabæk recognised Sverdrup's political genius and placed his organisation at Sverdrup's disposal.

This agreement laid the foundation of the *Liberal Party*[1]). Its platform had two main planks: 1) extension of the franchise and increased power for the elected bodies in the state as well as in local affairs, 2) full equality for Norway in the union and no steps towards a merging («amalgamation») of the two countries, rather a reduction of the partnership to the least possible degree. The Liberal Party was in opposition to the bureaucratic Cabinet then sitting, which, indeed, stood for liberalism in economic policy, but was conservative in constitutional matters and pro-

[1]) In Norway called "Venstre" (the "Left")

94

unionist. The supporters of the Cabinet formed the *Conservative Party*[1].) They wished to preserve the division of power established in the constitution and so repudiated parliamentary government. The Conservatives too claimed equality for Norway in the union, but they were inclined to extend the scope of the union and thus strengthen it. Many of them had been Scandinavianists and now saw a practical alternative to Scandinavian unity in a strengthening of the union with Sweden. The dominating personality on the Conservative side was the Prime Minister, *Frederik Stang*, an excellent lawyer, who for several years had been a very clever Minister for Home Affairs and had taken an especially active part in the development of communications. As Prime Minister for 20 years (1861—80) he took a strictly conservative stand in the political conflict and became more and more of a rigid bureaucrat.

The Liberal Party won its first victory in the first year of its existence, 1869, when it was enacted that the Storting in future was to meet every year (before this it only met every three years). This change made the Storting a more permanent factor in political life and increased its influence tremendously. Strangely enough this measure had been moved by the Cabinet, but the Conservative members of the Storting voted against it.

The second victory followed only two years later and was won on the union issue. A committee of Norwegians and Swedes had suggested a new union contract by which the union ties would be considerably strengthened. It was proposed to establish a union council and a union military force, and, last but not least, the Swedish Foreign Minister was to be recognised as common to both realms. The proposal met with violent opposition in Norway, and the Storting rejected it with an overwhelming majority, which included even many Conservative members.

But the main controversy came over a constitutional amendment. A private bill was introduced authorising Cabinet ministers

[2]) In Norway called "Høyre" (the "Right"). The two parties were not organised on a national basis till 1884.

to take part in the deliberations of the Storting. The bill was carried by three Stortings (in 1874, 1877 and 1880), with an increasing majority, but each time it was vetoed by the King on the advice of his Ministers. The Cabinet was not wholly unwilling to consent to the amendment but demanded in return certain conservative guarantees, which, however, the Liberals refused to accept, while Conservative Parliamentarians found them insufficient.

Sverdrup's great vision was to change the Cabinet Ministers from bureaucrats into politicians, from heads of the executive, who sat in their offices and remained there as long as it pleased the king, into political leaders, who met in the Storting for debate, worked in harmony with the majority there and were dependent on its confidence for being in office. "The division of power is nonsense", said Sverdrup. Although the amendment in itself did not establish parliamentary government, Sverdrup clearly saw this as a logical consequence. And so did the Cabinet and its supporters. The real issue was who was to have the power in the state, the king or the people. The controversy in the last stage came to centre round the question of the royal veto. The Conservatives asserted that in cases of constitutional amendments the king had an *absolute* veto, the Liberals that he had only a suspensive veto as in law cases, and some claimed, Jaabæk for instance, that he had no veto at all. In 1880, after the amendment had been carried a third time, the Storting passed a resolution declaring the amendment to be legally valid. But the Cabinet stubbornly refused to obey and did not appear in the Storting.

Johan Sverdrup saw only one way out of this impasse, to have the Cabinet Ministers sentenced to forfeit their offices through an impeachment, a trial before the Constitutional Court (in Norwegian "Riksrett"), which consists of the members of the Lagting and the judges of the Supreme Court. But he wanted to have the consent of the electors for such a step, and therefore postponed any further action till after the general elections of 1882.

After an election contest unsurpassed in Norwegian political history for passionate intensity, the Liberals won an overwhelming victory, 83 Liberal members being returned, against 31 Conservatives. After this the Cabinet was impeached, and after a trial found guilty of abuse of the royal veto and sentenced to forfeit their offices. The sentence was greeted with exultation by the Liberals, but with abhorrence by the Conservatives. The latter denounced it as a flagrant violation of justice. The procedure they declared to be a caricature and a disgraceful abuse of power.[1]) King Oscar, contrary to the hopes of many Conservatives, acquiesced in the sentence and dismissed the Cabinet, but he hesitated to call Johan Sverdrup into office. He made an attempt at governing with a moderately conservative Cabinet, but this proved a failure, and after a few months King Oscar had to swallow the bitter pill and request Sverdrup to form a Liberal Cabinet. Since then parliamentarism has been the political system of Norway, and has gradually been accepted by the whole nation.

Under the Sverdrup administration (1884—89), important reforms for the consolidation of democracy were achieved. The suffrage was extended, the jury system introduced for criminal cases mostly according to the English pattern, and the army was organised on a democratic and national basis. The elementary school system was highly improved and was left in the hands of popularly elected school boards.

A few years after the great victory, the Liberal party was split in a Moderate and a Radical wing. Sverdrup sided with the Moderates and experienced the tragedy of being forsaken

[1]) The basis of the latter contention was the fact that the Liberal Party had taken advantage of its overwhelming majority in the Storting to select on'y Liberals as members of the Lagting, contrary to the usual practice. The purpose was to obtain a conviction of the Cabinet by means of a Liberal majority in the Court. For it was supposed that the Supreme Court judges would vote for acquittal, which in fact they did. To-day it is generally admitted that the "Riksrett" was a *political* decision in a judicial form, but a necessary decision, many will add.

by the majority of his party. As a result of the Liberal split, the Conservative party had a renaissance and for a short time was in office under the premiership of *Emil Stang* (son of Frederik Stang), a clever Oslo lawyer, who had been Conservative Leader since 1882. He stood for a progressive conservatism, and therefore had some difficulties with the diehards in his party. From the beginning of the 90's the Liberal Party again had an absolute majority in the Storting and kept it till 1903, but there were changing Cabinets owing to the union conflicts.[1])

In this period the policy of democratic reform was carried on along the lines drawn up by Johan Sverdrup. Thus in 1898 *universal suffrage for men* was enacted, and only a few years later women too obtained a limited right to vote, *which was made universal in 1913.* Full democracy was thus established in Norway.

Meanwhile the working class had also organised itself politically by founding the *Norwegian Labour Party* in 1887. The new party soon adopted a socialist programme. As long as very few workers had the right to vote, however, there could be no chances for Labour candidates in the general elections, and therefore the Labour people supported the Liberal candidates. But after universal suffrage for men had been introduced, the Labour Party nominated its own candidates, and in 1903 succeeded in having 5 members elected to the Storting. In 1906 the number increased to 10 and in 1912 to 23 (out of 123).

8. *The Union Issue, 1890—1905.*

From the beginning of the 1890's foreign affairs assumed primary importance in Norwegian politics. The peace movement gathered momentum, but the union issue with Sweden was of still greater importance.

[1]) The Moderates had formed their own party, which mostly cooperated with the Conservatives. After the dissolution of the union in 1905 it disappeared.

For many years the poet *Bjørnstjerne Bjørnson* placed his dynamic personality at the service of the idea of peace and goodwill among nations. He carried on an intense propaganda in the country and exercised a great influence, also in political life. In 1890 the Norwegian Storting was the first parliament to pass (with a large majority) a resolution in favour of general arbitration treaties, and in the same year it sent delegates to the first universal Interparliamentary Conference, and was the only parliament which did so at public expense. In 1897, before the meeting of the first Hague Conference, the Storting again passed its resolution in favour of arbitration treaties, this time unanimously.

Thanks to this policy the Storting was entrusted with a highly honourable task in the work for peace. When the Swedish industrialist *Alfred Nobel* (the inventor of dynamite) in his will bequeathed his vast fortune to awards for achievements in literature and science, he included a prize for peace work. The awarding of this prize ("the Nobel peace prize") he left to a committee appointed by the Norwegian Storting. This committee began its work in 1901.

However, from the beginning of the 1890's the union problem was at the centre of Norwegian political life. The Liberal party set up a programme aiming at the establisment of an independent foreign service for Norway under the leadership of a Norwegian Foreign Minister. The Conservative party stood for establishing a union foreign service with equal right for Norwegians and Swedes to be Foreign Minister.

As a first step towards the realisation of their programme the Liberal majority in the Storting in 1892 passed a resolution by which an independent *consular service* was established, which they thought Norway had a right to do.[1]) But the King refused

---

[1]) The Conservative minority agreed with the Liberals concerning Norway's *right*. But they thought it would be wise to negotiate with Sweden. On the whole the Liberals in the union issue stood for one-sided Norwegian *action*, the Conservatives for *negotiation*.

to give his assent, maintaining that Norway had no right to establish her own consular service without previous agreement with Sweden. The Liberal Cabinet declared that it could not countersign a royal veto, and after some months of suspense the crisis terminated in the formation of a Conservative Cabinet. This Cabinet was only supported by a minority in the Storting and had constant trouble with the Liberal majority.

The Swedish authorities supported the attitude taken by the King. They demanded that the Storting should repeal its resolution of 1892, and proposed negotiations for a revision of the union contract. From certain quarters there were even heard voices threatening to use force against Norway. In face of the violent Swedish opposition and knowing that the military defence of Norway was in a poor state, the Storting found it necessary to make a retreat. On June 7th 1895, it resolved to open negotiations with Sweden concerning the whole union problem. After some years of deliberations it appeared impossible for the negotiators to reach an agreement. The Norwegian and Swedish viewpoints were totally different.

The defeat in the consular affair did not crush the national aspiration of the Norwegian people. But to the leaders it had now become clear that it was necessary to back up words with *military force*. Therefore, during the years before and after 1900 a strong rearmament took place. The navy was renewed and enlarged, coast defences were erected, the army was equipped with up-to-date artillery, and along the Swedish border the existing fortresses were modernised and new ones constructed. Both Liberal and Conservative politicians were active in the work of rearmament.

Meanwhile a change seemed to have taken place in the Swedish attitude to the Norwegian desire for a consular service of her own. The Swedish Government at the instigation of the Foreign Minister declared itself willing to discuss the establishment of a separate consular service for each of the two countries. Perhaps this change was due partly to the Norwegian rearmament, but probably also to fear of Russia, which at that time had started her encroachments in Finland. The possibility of Russian aggression against Scandinavia naturally made it desirable to establish good relations between Norway and Sweden. In any case, in spite of a certain scepticism within the Liberal Party, which was then in office, the negotiations started in 1902 and a preliminary result was reached the following year. But they ended in bitter disappointment for Norway. The Norwegian Cabinet was rather quick in bringing in its bill for an Act on the Consular Service, whereas the Swedish Cabinet hesitated. Not till the end of the year 1904 did its bill appear. And this bill, indeed, caused consternation in Norway. For it contained several clauses which in the Norwegian view were unacceptable to a sovereign state, as they would make Norway a dependency of Sweden.

It is probable that this change in the Swedish attitude also had an international background. The war between Russia and Japan which started in January 1904 and had caused great losses and serious defeats to Russia may have removed the fear of Russian aggression in Scandinavia and so reduced Sweden's interest in an agreement with Norway.

It goes without saying that bitterness was great in the whole nation, but above all in the Conservative party, which had wholeheartedly gone in for negotiation and believed in a good result. Everyone soon agreed that now the time had come for *action*, even if it should lead to the dissolution of the union. The consular issue had become a question of national prestige for Norway; the question was whether Norway was a sovereign state or not. When the Storting met after New Year 1905, long deliberations took place concerning the procedure to be adopted. At last it was agreed that a bill should be passed for the introduction of a wholly independent Norwegian Consular Service within a year.

The Conservative Cabinet, which had been in office since the autumn of 1903, resigned, and a Coalition Cabinet of Liberals,

Conservatives and Moderates took over in March. Its Prime Minister was *Christian Michelsen*, then 48 years old, an eminent and very wealthy shipowner from Bergen, who had taken an active part in the discussions concerning the consular issue in the 1890's, when he was a member of the Storting. He was a Liberal, but in the elections of 1903 he had, like several other Liberals, for various reasons joined hands with the Conservatives and formed a "United Party". After the election victory he became a member of the Conservative Cabinet. In fact, he was from the very start rather sceptical about the negotiations with Sweden, and after they had failed he broke away from the Cabinet. As Prime Minister he showed outstanding abilities as a leader, sound judgment, quick-wittedness and efficiency. In the events that followed, he became the admired leader and hero of the nation.

The bill for a Norwegian Consular Service was prepared by a special committee, and in May laid before the Odelsting and the Lagting. After a motion for postponement had been rejected against 6 votes, the bill was carried unanimously in both sections. But on May 27th King Oscar, as expected, vetoed the bill. The Norwegian Cabinet Section in Stockholm declared that it could not countersign the veto and handed in the resignations of the whole Cabinet. The King refused to accept the resignations on the ground that "no other ministry can now be formed."

The Cabinet Section then left for Oslo, where deliberations for further action took place during the following week. The King's words now proved fatal. Michelsen's political genius discovered in them a constitutional basis for declaring the union dissolved. Oscar II was King of Norway no longer, since according to the constitution he could exercise his royal functions only through a responsible Cabinet, and now he lacked one. When Norway and Sweden had no king in common, it followed as a logical conclusion that there was no union between them any more. On the morning of the 7th of June the Storting unanimously passed a resolution declaring that the union had ceased to exist, and authorised the Cabinet to continue in office and rule the country. In the same sitting the Storting passed an address to King Oscar, in which he was requested to permit a prince of the Bernadotte dynasty to ascend the throne of Norway ("the Bernadotte offer"). This address was not answered by the King until several months later, but at once he protested vehemently against the resolution of the Storting concerning the union.

The Swedish Diet, which met in an extraordinary session soon afterwards, declared unanimously that it could not admit the right of the Storting to act as it had done. But it added that if the Norwegian people through new elections or a plebiscite expressed its adherence to the Storting, the Diet was willing to negotiate for a dissolution of the union, on certain conditions. Before this was publicly known in Norway, the Norwegian Government itself proposed a plebiscite, and the Storting accepted it. The plebiscite was held in August and showed a practically unanimous support of the 7th June resolution (only 184 votes against).

Then negotiations took place throughout September, and after many difficulties and critical situations agreement was reached. The agreement was accepted by the Storting and the Diet with an overwhelming majority.

Thus, fortunately, the union between the two Scandinavian countries was dissolved in peace and then Norway was recognised as a wholly independent state, by Sweden and by all other countries.

But another question remained to be settled, that of the future constitution of Norway. The Bernadotte offer was now formally refused by King Oscar. As this had been foreseen, the Norwegian Government had, in the course of the summer, by means of special ambassadors secretly made contact with Prins *Carl* of Denmark (second eldest grandson of Christian IX, married to Princess *Maud*, daughter of the British King Edward VII). Now this was made public. But it soon appeared that many wanted to abolish the monarchy and establish a republic, among

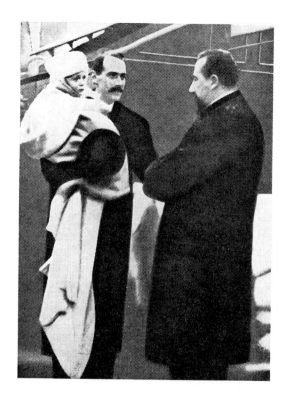

The Prime Minister Christian Michelsen welcoming the new king, Haakon VII, in 1905. The boy is Olav, the present King of Norway.

them several members of the Storting, and even one of the Ministers, who subsequently had to resign. Prince Carl firmly declared that he wanted to know where the Norwegian people stood before he could accept the Norwegian crown. Consequently a new plebescite was held, in November. It had the result that a vast majority voted for monarchy (260,000 versus ca. 70,000).

Then the Storting unanimously elected Prince Carl King of Norway, and he took the name of *Haakon VII*, thus linking up with the old line of Norwegian kings. Next year the new King and Queen were crowned in the ancient cathedral of Trondheim.

9. *Cultural Life.*

In several fields Norwegian culture experienced a true renaissance from the middle of the 19th century onward.

In the field of literature, the name which became most widely known was probably that of the playwright *Henrik Ibsen* (1828—1906). The dour air which surrounds so much that Ibsen wrote is supposed to reflect something that is characteristically Norwegian, but, like most attempts at national identification, this is not a particularly convincing generalisation. Ibsen was a European, an international figure, although many of his plays had a specifically Norwegian theme, and nearly all had a Norwegian domestic setting. Like many a great artist, Ibsen may seem contradictory in much that he wrote, but then he did not tie himself to the enunciation of any particular programme; he simply sought by the power of his pungent, provocative playwright's pen to peel off some of the layers that swaddle the pith of the human condition and human society. In the plush of the late Victorian era he was an important disruptive force. He was battered by the critics, but won through. To-day, in an iconoclastic age, his ideas raise less of a stir, but his craft as a playwright and his personification of the abstract in a deep perspective are as effective as ever. His combination of realism and poetic symbolism is masterly. The scene on the stage may be a drawing room, but the thundering world is always there, waiting to break in. As a rule his women cut a more heroic figure than the men, and Nora, Hedvig, Hedda Gabler, and Rebecca West are favourite roles of actresses everywhere.

Ibsen looms supreme to-day, but in his time there was a rich crop of writers of high rank. Novelists like *Alexander Kielland* and *Jonas Lie* may be mentioned, and above all *Bjørnstjerne Bjørnson* (1832—1910), a great-hearted patriot and poet, novelist and playwright, a patriarch and public orator of his nation. In particular he lives in the minds of the Norwegian people as the author of the national anthem.

Well-known novelists of a later period are *Sigrid Undset* (1882—1949) and *Knut Hamsun* (1859—1952), both, like Bjørnson, winners of the Nobel prize for literature.

In the field of pictorial art *Edvard Munch* (1863—1944) was one of the founders and foremost exponents of the international expressionist school. Technically his bold use of colour and the continuous sweeping flow of his brush are distinguishing features of much of his work. His choice of theme was often original, sombrely even morbidly dramatic at times, at other times tender and evocative. He was loath to part with his canvases, and at his death he bequeathed several thousand paintings, drawings and etchings to the city of Oslo. A gallery containing this unique collection was opened in 1963. A great sculptor was *Gustav Vigeland* (1869—1943), who also left most of his works to the city of Oslo.

The name best known in the field of Norwegian music is still that of *Edvard Grieg* (1843—1907). Much of his inspiration he took from the folk tunes of his country, melodies that had been preserved for centuries. Grieg was particularly a master of the miniature.

In science there are also names of note such as those of *Niels Henrik Abel* (1802—1829), the mathematician, and *Dr. Armauer Hansen* (1841—1912), discoverer of the leprosy bacillus. Medical science has made continual progress. While the average span of life for a Norwegian at the beginning of the present century was around 55 years, it is now well over 70.

In the technological sphere several inventions could be mentioned. Of particular importance was an arc-furnace developed by *K. Birkeland* (professor of physics at the University of Oslo(and *Sam. Eyde* (engineer and industrialist) at the beginning of the century for the large-scale production of artificial fertilizer out of air with the aid of electric power. This opened the era of modern industry in Norway.

VIII. INDEPENDENT NORWAY

1. *The Concession Laws.*

The first 50 years of full Norwegian independence were characterised by the rapid transformation of the country from a mainly agricultural into a mainly manufacturing and trading society, to a great extent by means of foreign capital. This was not a totally new departure, but an important new feature was the rise of metallurgical and chemical industries and the use of electricity as energy. The cheapest way of producing electricity was by harnessing the waterfalls and building power plants there. This gave Norway new chances for further industrialisation, as the country was rich in natural waterfalls, and moreover artificial waterfalls could easily be created.

Therefore many foreign industrialists became interested in buying waterfalls and lakes, and also mining properties and the forests attracted the attention of business men, Norwegians as well as foreigners. This caused uneasiness and fear in many circles. It looked as if a large part of Norway's natural resources before long might fall into the hands of foreigners and the new-born national liberty would thus be threatened. For this reason it was thought necessary for the Government to interfere and to control these trends by legislation. Most responsible politicians agreed to this fundamental view[1]), and thus arose the *concession laws*, which established the principle of Government consent for the acquisition of waterfalls and mines and in certain cases also

[1]) Among them was Michelsen, who continued in office as Prime Minister till the autumn of 1907, when he resigned for reasons of health. He died in 1925.

of forests. Foreigners were even forbidden to purchase forest lands in Norway.

As to the details, however, opinions differed very much, and the concession policy was the main political issue between 1905 and the outbreak of World War I. The Liberal Party, which had gained a solid majority in the elections of 1906, was split over this issue. The majority stood for rather rigid provisions, especially in the law regarding waterfalls. The most controversial provision in the Act was the so called "reversion right", which implied that the waterfall and the power plant at the expiration of the concession term (60 to 80 years) were to become Government property without any compensation to the owners. This provision applied to all stock companies, Norwegian as well as foreign.

The Conservatives and the minority Liberals (who soon formed their own party called the "Independent Left") stood for more moderate concession laws, especially for easier conditions for Norwegian or Norwegian controlled companies.

It was in the year 1909 that the concession laws in their final form were carried in the Storting by the combined votes of the (majority) Liberals and the Labour members. The Liberals were then in office under *Gunnar Knudsen*, a versatile business man (ship-owner, industrialist and landowner), who had taken an active part in politics since the beginning of the 1890's. He had been a member of the Michelsen Cabinet in 1905, as Minister of Finance, but resigned in the autumn because he was a republican. He was no great orator, but a commanding personality who had his party well in hand.

In the elections of 1909 the Conservatives and Independents won a slight victory and came into office, but no alterations were made in the concession laws, because several of the Independents were against altering them. The elections of 1912 returned a solid Liberal majority, and Gunnar Knudsen again became Prime Minister and remained in office until 1920. The concession laws remained in force and were even intensified on some points.

2. Towards the Welfare State.

The industrial revolution created an increasing number of factory workers, who naturally organised themselves in trade unions to protect or promote their interests. The first trade unions grew up in the 1870's, and in 1899 they were joined in a *"National Federation of Trade Unions."*[1])

But the conditions of the working class also called for the interference of the Government. It was in fact the Conservative Cabinet in the 1870's that took the initiative in this field by setting forth proposals for the protection of child labour in factories. To these proposals the Liberals took a rather negative attitude. They were as yet Manchester liberals, and it was above all the great constitutional conflict that occupied their minds. But after the victory in 1884 the new Liberal Cabinet under Johan Sverdrup appointed a commission representing many groups and interests to consider a wide range of labour problems. The first practical results of their deliberations were two laws, the *Factory Inspection Act* (1892) and the *Accidents Insurance Act* (1894). The former established state inspection of all factories, forbade the employment of children in factories and regulated night work and holiday work. The latter established state insurance against disabilities caused by accidents in factories and thus was the first social security measure in Norway.

But the great age of labour legislation came with the 20th century. The period from 1906 to 1919 was in fact the first golden era of social reform policy. In those years the foundation was laid of the modern welfare state in Norway, which was fully developed under the Labour administration in the years before and after the German occupation. In the first place the Acts passed in the 1890's were revised and extended several times, anp next a series of new laws were passed which introduced a health insurance scheme, established maximum working hours, even

[1]) Next year the employers formed a *"Norwegian Employers' Association"*.

Plant for the production of artificial fertilizers at Glomfjord.

in the merchant marine, established a bank to assist workers in the purchase of homes and plots of ground, and last but not least, a law was passed for the peaceful settlement of labour disputes.

People of all parties were active in this legislation, but the most prominent part was played by *Johan Castberg*, a lawyer on the left wing of the Liberal Party, who also had a leading hand in the framing of the concession laws as well as laws concerning maternity welfare and the rights of illegitimate children.

3. *Norway and World War I.*

At the outbreak of the First World War, in August 1914, all three Scandinavian countries declared themselves neutral and cooperated closely for the maintenance of neutrality throughout the war years. This cooperation began officially with a meeting of the three kings at Malmö (in Sweden) in December 1914, and in the course of the following years the kings and the statesmen met for conferences.

In spite of many difficulties and some acute conflicts with Germany and Great Britain, mainly concerning the export trade and submarine warfare, Norway managed to keep out of the war, thanks to the diplomatic skill displayed by the Foreign Minister, *N. C. Ihlen*, and the strengthening of the military defence carried out during the war which made it possible to keep an efficient neutrality defence guard. It is an established fact that in the autumn of 1916, in connection with a controversy over submarine warfare, the German government seriously considered declaring war on Norway. But the military authorities in Germany, after evaluating Norway's military strength, found that Germany would lose more than she would gain by adding Norway to the number of her enemies and so the controversy was settled peacefully and favourably to Norway.

But the effects of the war on life in Norway were in many ways disastrous. Owing to the British blockade and the German submarine warfare the importation of foodstuffs and other necessities was heavily reduced, so that certain articles had to be rationed. Prices rose, to begin with rather slowly, but during the last two years of the war and the first two years after the war they rose very rapidly. The top level was reached in the autumn of 1920, and was nearly four times higher than pre-war level. This inflation was due not only to the shortage of commodities, but also to an abundance of money as compared with the quantity of commodities Shortly after the outbreak of the war, the Bank of Norway abolished the redemption duty, thus leaving the gold standard, and during the years that followed the quantity of bank-notes was many-doubled. But wages kept very slow pace with the rise in prices, and wage-earners were therefore very badly off.

On the other hand ship-owners and exporters had large profits. As in previous wars there was a great demand for tonnage, and

Norwegian ships were hired by the Allied Powers at high rates. New shipping companies were started, often by inexperienced people, but as long as the boom lasted they all gave large dividends. This caused wild speculation on the stock exchange. Many people became rich in a hurry, but when the slump set in, after 1920, their wealth dwindled or even disappeared rather quickly.

4. *Arctic Expansion.*

The general feeling in Norway had been on the Allied side in the war, and practically all the merchant marine had been in the service of the Western Powers, especially of Great Britain. After the war Norway presented a claim to the victors for the Arctic islands of Spitzbergen and Bear Island, and was supported by Denmark and Sweden. In acknowledgement of the great services which Norwegian shipping had rendered the Allied cause, Norway's claim was granted. From the year 1925 the islands came under Norwegian sovereignty and were given the name of *Svalbard.* On the other hand the Norwegian Government undertook to respect the foreign economic interests established there. Some years later *Jan Mayen Island* in the Arctic and *Peter I's Island* and *Bouvet Island* in the Antarctic were also annexed by Norway without meeting any protests from other powers. And lastly, in 1939, a part of the Antarctic continent called *Queen Maud Land* was placed under Norwegian sovereignty. It was the whaling there that caused Norway to take an interest in these regions. An additional reason was the fact that *Roald Amundsen,* Norway's great geographical explorer, had planted the Norwegian flag on the South Pole in 1911, and later several Norwegian expeditions had been active in the exploration of the Antarctic regions.

It may be added that Norwegian explorers have also been active in other parts of the world. The best known among recent expeditions is perhaps the one carried out by *Thor Heyerdahl* in 1947. With five companions he drifted on a wooden raft, called

112

the Kon-Tiki, across the Pacific Ocean from Peru, to find support for his theory that the Polynesians originally came from South America in prehistoric times.

5. Norway in the League of Nations.

The *League of Nations* was established in 1920 as an instrument for peace and international justice. In line with her traditions in this field Norway joined the League. It was very fortunate that the country was able to send one of its most illustrious sons, *Dr. Fridtjof Nansen*, as a member of the Norwegian delegation to the Assembly as long as he lived (until 1930). Thanks to his lofty idealism, untiring energy and dauntless courage, Norway obtained a highly respected position in the League. Nansen placed his dynamic personality and his warm heart at the service of the work for peace and humanitarian relief carried on or supported by the League of Nations.

It was a great advantage that Nansen had a world-wide renown as a scholar and geographical explorer. His first feat as an explorer he performed in 1888 when he crossed Greenland on skis. Then came his push towards the North Pole. In 1893 he set off with a crew of sturdy seamen on board the *"Fram"*, and sailed along the northern coast of Asia in the hope of drifting across the Pole. Finding that he had miscalculated, he left the ship with one of his men and attempted to get to the Pole on skis. He had to turn back at 86° 14' north, and so failed to reach his goal. But he had got farther north than any explorer before him, and the observations he made were extremely valuable for later explorations in the Arctic regions. And above all, he and his men had set an example of hardihood, strength and perseverance, of viking spirit displayed in a new type of achievement. After the "Fram" expedition Nansen was appointed professor of oceanography at the University of Oslo, and did excellent work in the organisation of this new branch of science.

Soon new fields of activity opened up for him. In 1905, during the union conflict, he rendered great services to his country by pleading Norway's cause in the world press, and for some years afterwards he was Norway's first ambassador in London.

During World War I he was sent to USA by the Norwegian Government to negotiate an agreement for the importation of foodstuffs to blockaded Norway, and obtained very satisfactory results.

But his greatest achievements he performed in the 1920's partly in the service of the League of Nations, partly on his own responsibility. He organised the repatriation of half a million prisoners of war from Russia and Siberia, the settlement of one and a half million Russian political refugees, and later other refugees. Thousands of people owe their lives to the "Nansen passport". Thanks to the relief work he set on foot, millions of lives were saved during the great famine in Russia. He directed the exchange of two million inhabitants between Greece and Turkey and made efforts for the settlement of the homeless Armenians. In all this work he showed outstanding skill as an organiser and administrator.

In the 1930's *C. J. Hambro* (newspaper editor, literary critic and author), for many years Leader of the Conservative Party and Speaker of the Storting, was a permanent member of the Norwegian delegation. Through his brilliant eloquence and extraordinary energy he obtained an influential position in the League of Nations.

6. *Economic and Political Unrest.*

The war boom came to an end late in the autumn of 1920. Then a slump began, partly owing to world conditions, partly as a result of a conscious and planned deflation policy on the part of the Bank of Norway, which by this time had got a new governor. Between 1921 and 1928 the rate of the krone rose, with some fluctuations, from less than half to par value, and the gold standard was reintroduced in 1928.

This period was filled with economic and social unrest, marketing difficulties, which caused a decrease in production in the export industries, low shipping rates, bankruptcies, unemployment and labour conflicts. Practically all producers had debts, to a great extent contracted in the boom period. To all of them, but particularly to the farmers, the fall in prices that followed the rise in the value of the krone made the burden of debt heavier and so increased their difficulties.

Fortunately the reintroduction of the gold standard took place at a time of growing prosperity in the world at large. The years that followed were, therefore, marked by stability and fairly good conditions in Norway. But then, in 1931, the effects of the great economic world crisis reached the country and led to a new slump, harder than that of the twenties. Farmers were faced with low prices for their products and heavy debts. A great number of them lost their farms through the execution of enforced sales and there was a feeling of panic and revolt among them. Forestry and manufactures suffered badly, and the number of unemployed workers reached an unprecedented height. In some places there were labour conflicts which gave expression to bitter class animosity, and armed conflicts often seemed imminent.

At the very start of the crisis the Bank of Norway found it necessary to follow the example of Great Britain and leave the gold standard. Norway thus again had a paper currency, and the gold standard has not been reintroduced so far.

Fortunately the period of severe depression did not last very long. In 1934 things slowly began to improve, in Norway as in other European countries. In the course of the next few years the change became more evident, and the last few years before the Second World War were even fairly good. The economic policy pursued by the Government had some share in this development.

7. *Party Divisions.*

In the inter-war period several political parties had a turn in office, since there was no single party with an absolute majority in the Storting. In 1921 a new party emerged, the *Farmers'*

Party[1]), which absorbed votes from both the Liberals and the Conservatives. For most of the time up to 1935 the Liberal Party was in office, largely because it had an intermediate position and often had the support of one or more of the extreme parties. During the First World War, the Labour Party became strongly radical, and the radical elements, who had communist sympathies and believed in revolution as a means of achieving power, took over the Party leadership in 1918. Shortly afterwards the Labour Party joined the Third International and accepted its principles, the so-called "Moscow theses", according to which dictatorship was the form of government to be established. This led the moderate wing to break away and form a separate party, the *Norwegian Social Democratic Labour Party.* Soon afterwards the majority of the Labour Party broke with Moscow, though they still kept their revolutionary programme. The remaining minority then formed the *Norwegian Communist Party.* These three working-class parties fought each other bitterly for several years. But then the Labour Party and the Social Democrats merged into one party, and this new party made great progress at the elections of 1927 and made up the largest group in the Storting (59 members out of 150). The Communist Party lost strength and was soon without representatives in the Storting.

After a reverse in 1930, the Labour Party made further gains at the next two elections. The Party had now abandoned its revolutionary programme. It made *democracy* its basic principle and went in for a policy of social welfare as well as practical measures for the reduction of unemployment. In 1936 it had 70 representatives elected. In 1935 the Labour Party and the Farmers' Party had joined hands in order to overthrow *Mowinckel's*[2]) Liberal Government, which they thought was doing

[1]) In 1959 it changed its name to the *Centre Party.*

[2]) J. L. Mowinckel was a wealthy ship-owner from Bergen who first became a member of the Storting in 1906 and soon came to the fore in the Liberal Party. In the inter-war period he was Prime Minister three times.

too little to help the unemployed and to provide the farmers with better prices for their products and alleviate the burden of their debts. Then a Labour Government was formed with *Johan Nygaardsvold* as Prime Minister.

Nygaardsvold was a saw-mill worker from the Trondheim area, who had been a member of the Storting since 1916. Through his native intelligence, sound judgment, and upright character, he had won a highly respected position in the Storting. From an early age he had spent his leisure hours reading history and literature. In addition, thanks to a five years' stay in USA, he had acquired a good command of the English language. The office of Foreign Minister in this Government was held by the eminent historian, Dr. *Halvdan Koht*. He was Professor of History at the University of Oslo, and for many years he had held a leading position in the International Organisation of Historians and at home had engaged in a many-sided cultural activity. In politics he had taken an active part in local affairs, as member of a District Council near Oslo.

Under the Nygaardsvold administration, increased grants were voted to public works and farmers were given better prices for their products and easier terms if they were in debt. The National Budget rose sharply, and it became necessary to impose new taxes, including purchase tax. But each year the national accounts showed a credit balance. The policy of social reform was now carried on further. Through the *Labour Protection Act* of 1936, workers and staff in all professions achieved greater security than ever before and a new feature was that all were guaranteed, by law, *holidays with full pay. Old age pensions,* a social reform which had long been prepared, were introduced in the same year with the support of all parties, and in the post-war years extended so as to comprise everybody regardless of financial status. Just before the war, the Storting passed, with Labour and Liberal support, another new social reform, *unemployment insurance.*

Before the Labour Party came to power, it had opposed military defence and had voted against the defence budget.

Now it changed its views and itself voted grants for defence. After the First World War the Norwegian military forces were very much reduced, partly because it was necessary to cut down expenditure on all sides, partly because many had hopes that the League of Nations would succeed in creating an age of peace and goodwill in the world. But these hopes faded fast during the thirties, and in the last few years before the outbreak of the next World War grants for defence were increased. All parties in the Storting voted for these grants, but many believed that far too little was being spent on defence.

Major *Vidkun Quisling*, who had for a short while been Minister of Defence in a Government for the Farmers' Party, founded in 1933 a new party, National Unity ("Nasjonal Samling"). Its programme was strongly influenced by fascist and national-socialist ideas. It took part in the Storting elections of 1933 and 1936, but obtained only about 2 per cent of the votes cast and got no representatives in the Storting. After its second electoral defeat in 1936, Quisling's party practically disintegrated.

8. *War and Occupation (1940—1945).*

When the Second World War broke out in 1939, Norway declared herself neutral and managed to keep out of the war until the following April, in spite of certain encroachments on her neutrality made by both the Germans and the British. After the Germans had concluded the campaign against Poland, several months passed without major hostilities. Everyone waited in anxious expectancy to see where the blow would fall in the spring. There were several indications that it could be in Scandinavia. For the Western Powers it was thought vital to put a stop to the Swedish export of iron ore to Germany via the port of Narvik in North Norway, and by a group in the German Naval High Command it was considered as very important to secure a mastery of the Norwegian coastline, particularly because airfields and submarine bases in Norway would be of great help in the battle against Britain.

118

In Germany it was Grand Admiral *Raeder* who took up the idea of an attack on Norway. From the beginning of October he began to put pressure on Hitler, but received little encouragement. Hitler wished to concentrate his forces in a grand western offensive aiming at the defeat of France, and he reckoned that this offensive could be launched in the autumn of 1939. When it became clear that the offensive would have to be postponed till the spring, he showed a more positive interest. But it was only when Raeder managed to get support from a Norwegian quarter that Hitler was converted to the idea. In December Vidkun Quisling came to Berlin and was introduced to Hitler by Admiral Raeder. There was a great danger, Quisling contended, that the British would establish themselves in Norway with the consent of the Norwegian Government. This made Hitler seriously consider the question of occupying the country.

In Great Britain *Winston Churchill* (then First Lord of the Admiralty) took the initiative in the matter of Norway. At the end of September 1939 he submitted to the British Cabinet a proposal for laying mines along the western coast of Norway in order to force the German ships carrying iron ore to move out on the high seas. He did not gain the support of the Government either then or later in the autumn, when he took up the matter again. It was not until December that the British Government agreed to submit the plan to their military authorities for expert consideration, and by then the question of help to Finland in the war against Soviet Russia had also arisen and complicated matters.

In the course of the next few months, deliberations and laying of plans were taking place on both sides. In Germany this happened in deepest secrecy, while the Western Powers in the course of their consultations sent a series of appeals and warnings to the Norwegian and Swedish Governments. The Norwegian Government was bent on maintaining a policy of strict neutrality and worded very strong protests against threats and violations of neutrality from any quarter. In this war, too, a neutrality protection guard was set up along the coast, but it was considerably weaker than in the First World War.

During the first few days of April, both Germany and Great Britain were engaged in preparing military operations against Norway. On the morning of April 8th, the British laid mines in Norwegian territorial waters, and preparations had been made for occupying special points along the Norwegian coast in case Germany reacted to the mine-laying operations by attacking Norway or by making a move in this direction. The British expected a reaction of this kind from the Germans and they reckoned on being able to make their own landings with the consent of the Norwegians. Consequently their landing troops had little equipment and in reality were never sent at all. For in the meantime the Germans were already on their way northwards with the aim of occupying Norway.

Early on the morning of the 9th of April, shortly after midnight, the attack was launched. In the course of the morning German troops succeeded in occupying the major ports as far north as Narvik, and began to invade the country. Around New Year 1940, the defence forces of North Norway had been partly mobilised as a result of the outbreak of the Finnish-Russian War. But in South Norway little had been done to build up a state of military preparedness. The land lay practically open to attack when the enemy came.

Soon after midnight the members of the Government came together and at once resolved to order mobilisation. The meeting continued for the rest of the night. At 5 o'clock the German minister in Oslo appeared and handed over to the Foreign Minister an ultimatum demanding the acceptance of a German military and administrative occupation of the country. The ultimatum was unanimously rejected by the Government. The King, who was not present at the meeting, was informed by telephone and gave his consent. From that moment Norway was in fact at war with Germany. At a meeting of King and Government which took place at Hamar later in the morning,

120

C. J. Hambro (1885—1964)
Member of the Storting
1919—1957,
speakes 1926—45.

the state of war was declared by *Order in Council* and thus received a constitutional sanction.

Shortly after 7 o'clock the King and the royal family, the Government and the members of the Storting had left the capital and gone by train up to *Hamar* and later to *Elverum*, some 60 miles north-east of Oslo. This evacuation was the result of the initiative of the Speaker of the Storting, *C. J. Hambro*, who in this critical situation displayed a wonderful quick-wittedness and energy. It was largely to his credit that the King and the Government were saved from falling into the hands of the Germans. But a war episode also helped to make possible this fortunate escape. The German cruiser *Blücher* which, together with other warships, was forcing its way up the Oslo fjord, was sunk in the narrow sound at *Dröbak*, and a thousand men were drowned. The other ships turned and landed their troops farther south. Thus the naval push toward Oslo had failed, and the occupation of the capital was retarded by several hours.

121

That same morning the gold reserves of the Bank of Norway (worth 240 million kroner) were carried away from Oslo in motor lorries. Later on they were, in many ingenious ways, transported farther north' and at last came safely across the ocean to America.

The order for mobilisation had meanwhile been sent out, but it proved impossible to get the entire Norwegian army mobilised at such short notice, and though the Norwegian troops put up a determined show in many places, they lacked training and were heavily outnumbered. The British troops which arrived ten days later to help at the front were inexperienced and poorly equipped. In the course of a month the country was in the hands of the Germans as far north as the county of North Tröndelag. The British expeditionary forces had by that time been called home. In North Norway it was possible to organise a better defence owing to the partial mobilisation around the New Year, and fighting continued there for another month. The German advance was stopped north of Narvik, and this town was recaptured. British naval forces and French and Polish army troops assisted here, but owing to developments on the French front these troops were also recalled at the beginning of June. The King and the Government then found themselves obliged to give up the fight in Norway, and on June 7th they crossed to England in order to carry on the struggle for Norway's freedom from there. This step was in accordance with a final resolution of the Storting (on April 9th at Elverum) which gave the Government the authority to continue waging war against Germany, if necessary beyond the borders of the country. Soon thousands of young Norwegians streamed across to Great Britain, often by way of Sweden. In Great Britain a Norwegian army was established and a Norwegian air force and navy built up. In May 1945 the total Norwegian forces in Great Britain numbered 15 000 men. The Norwegian merchant marine, most of which was on the high seas when the war broke out, did magnificent work conveying supplies for the allies. But this was at the

122

cost of some 4000 seamen's lives, and about half the fleet was sunk.

During its sittings at Hamar on April 9th, the Storting heard reports from the Government concerning the events of the preceding night and was also informed that the members of the Government had handed in their resignations to the King that same morning. The Storting then *unanimously* passed a resolution which requested the Government to continue in office, but added that some new consultative members, belonging to the opposition, should be appointed. This was done, and thus a coalition government was formed. Some months after the Government's arrival in London, Koht resigned as Foreign Minister and was replaced by *Trygve Lie*, also a Labour Party man, who had been a member of the Nygaardsvold Government from the very start, first as Minister of Justice (he was a lawyer), then as Minister of Trade, and after the outbreak of the World War, as Minister of Supplies. In all these offices he had shown great energy and eminent ability as an administrator.

On the afternoon of the first day of the German invasion of Norway, Vidkun Quisling announced over the Oslo radio that he had formed a new Government with himself at the head, and he issued orders for a cease-fire. This, however, led to a more determined resistance on the part of the Norwegians. Hitler required King Haakon to recognise Quisling as Prime Minister, but the King categorically refused, with the support of his Government.

Quisling's dramatic announcement on the radio created a world-wide sensation and was generally believed to be part of a deeplaid plan engineered by Hitler, his Foreign Ministry, and his military leaders. The belief was mistaken, however. Grand Admiral Raeder had found Quisling a convenient instrument in December, 1939, when he made Hitler interested in the plan to attack Norway, but the German military leaders did not intend to make any further use of him. They well knew that

Quisling's supporters were only a handful of insignificant people, that his so-called party was virtually non-existent. The German plan was to take the Norwegian capital by surprise and force the Government to surrender and collaborate. However, the unexpected escape of the King and the Government from Oslo at the moment of invasion created a new situation. Quisling seized the opportunity of proclaiming himself "Prime Minister" and Hitler, furious that the Norwegian Government had wrecked the original German plan, decided to back him.

The backing which Quisling received at this moment was not very strong, however. Reports kept coming in at the German headquarters indicating that the new "Head of Government" was being indignantly rejected by his countrymen. There could be no doubt that his spectacular treachery had strengthened the Norwegian will to resist. After a few days the Germans in Oslo drew the logical conclusion. On April 15th they forced Quisling to resign.

An *Administrative Council* for the occupied sections of the country was set up, and some days later *Josef Terboven* was appointed "Reichskommissar für die besetzten Norwegischen Gebiete". The Administrative Council was composed of prominent government officials, all of them loyal to the King and the constitutional government. Terboven was supposed to safeguard German interests in Norway, but after the Germans had occupied all Norway he had in fact supreme authority in the country. In the course of time he had sent up from Germany a large staff of officials and police ("Gestapo"). After the King and the Government had left Norway, negotiations took place between the Reichskommissar and those members of the Storting who were still in Norway concerning the establishment of a new system of government. These negotiations led nowhere, and while they were going on Quisling was at work behind the scene attempting to come to power once more. Finally he persuaded the German authorities to declare that his national-socialist party, "National Unity", was the one official party and that the way to Norwegian independence was for the Norwegian people to join this party. All other political parties were prohibited. On September 25th the Administrative Council was replaced by a group of so-called "commissar councillors", who were to be in charge of the various Government departments. Quisling was not included in this group, but continued as Leader ("Förer") of his Party and in this capacity achieved a prominent position in the state. An immediate consequence of the new system of government was that the supreme court judges resigned from their posts, and new judges were nominated, all of whom belonged to the Quisling Party. On February 1st 1942 the system underwent a further change. The commissar councillors were from then onwards to form a Government and be known as Ministers, and Quisling now participated in the Government as its head and bore the title of President Minister. It was stated that this was to be a real step towards restoring full independence for Norway, and the new order was made known by a solemn act of state at Akershus Castle in Oslo. In reality conditions were exactly the same as before. The Germans ruled the country.

Quisling's plan was to build up a new constitution, based on the so-called "principle of authority and responsibility". This meant that the various decisions in the state, and also in each of the counties and local districts were to be made by one man, and he was responsible to the Government department which had *nominated* him. In addition he was to have an advisory assembly, which was also nominated. All elections were therefore abolished. Quisling began with the county and district authorities and in due course there were nominated new county governors ("fylkesmenn") and local mayors, and of these as many as possible were members of the Quisling Party. In the central Government the Norwegian "Förer" was to make decisions in consultation with a national assembly called the *Riksting*, to be composed of nominated representatives for the various trades and professions which were to be organised in large "associations".

But when this part of the plan was to be set into operation in the winter of 1942, there was violent opposition. A beginning was made with the schoolteachers, but nearly all of them refused to become members of the "Teachers' Association". Over a thousand of them were arrested and sent to concentration camps, mostly to *Kirkenes* in Finnmark. But the general resistance could not be broken. The other professions followed the teachers' example to a man, and the plan for a "Riksting" was never put into execution.

The new Government also came into sharp conflict with the Church. Again and again the bishops conducted strongly worded campaigns in their pastoral letters against the principles and practices of the "new era". Fina'ly, the Bishop of Oslo, *Eivind Berggrav*, was removed from his see, and then the other bishops and nearly all the clergy resigned from their posts, but continued working under a temporary church leadership. Bishop Berggrav was interned shortly afterwards, and the same happened in due course to the other bishops and a large number of the clergy. Other clergymen were forced to move from their parishes.

The Germans and the Quisling Party felt considerable irritation because they secured so little support and even encountered strong opposition from the University of Oslo. First they arrested the Rector of the University, Professor *D.A. Seip*, and sent him to Germany. Later they closed the University and sent several hundred students to Germany as prisoners.

To make the Party stronger and more effective, uniformed troops, known as the "hird", were formed within the framework of the Quisling Party. To begin with the "hird" divisions were unarmed and mostly used for parades. Later they were armed and received training in the use of arms.

In spite of intense propaganda, of pressure and threats on the one hand and enticing rewards in the form of official posts and power on the other, the Quisling Party never succeeded in gaining solid support. Almost all the people in Norway were in

126

opposition to the Party, partly because they regarded the relations of the Party with the Germans as treason, partly because national socialist ideology struck no roots among the people. It was especially the imposition of a dictatorship and the abolition of freedom of utterance which provoked a sharp general reaction. All open resistance was forbidden by the new authorities. But in secrecy a widespread information service was zealously organised. Secret newspapers circulated in large numbers and brought news from the war outside and the struggle in Norway, as well as reliable reports on current questions. Secret military forces were also organised and weapons were collected for use on the day when the war of liberation would begin in Norway. Some of these troops were trained as sabotage groups, and their function was to destroy industrial plants which were feeding the German war machine. In this work they often received help from specially trained Norwegian units sent over from Great Britain. Also in Sweden Norwegian military units under the name of "police troops" were organised.

For taking part in this struggle, some 35,000 Norwegians were sent to prison. Many of them suffered torture, and several hundred were killed. A great number were transported to concentration camps in Germany, and of these some 1400 died through starvation, torture, and ill-treatment. Among those deported were 760 Jews, men, women and children, more than half the Jewish population of Norway, the remainder having escaped to Sweden. Only 22 came back from Germany, the others had practically all been killed in the gas chambers.

The will to resist was not destroyed among the Norwegian people, and splendid solidarity and comradeship were displayed. This was especially the case among young people. The Nazis tried to get all sports organisations under their control, but met with a stubborn united front and had to give up. Sportsmen and athletes refused to take part in public competitions. No more successful was the attempt to mobilise Norwegian youth for a labour corps to work for the Germans under the name of

May 1945. German officers surrender the Castle of Akershus to Norwegian home forces.

"national labour service". Only a few allowed themselves to be enrolled, and thousands of young boys hid in the forests in order to escape being rounded up by the police. From the autumn of 1944, all organised resistance work in Norway was placed under one command, the "Home Front Command". Its head was the President of the pre-war Supreme Court, *Paal Berg*, a fact which was of course not generally known until after the war.

Besides the political struggle, the Norwegian people also had a hard struggle during these years to keep body and soul together. Provisions ran very short, and much of the country's own produce went to the occupying forces. In due course almost all foodstuffs were rationed, and rations were very small indeed. Even fish was scarce. The supply of clothing, shoes, and other commodities also diminished. With these conditions, sale of goods took place largely in the form of exchange. But the people at large

128

King Haakon sets foot on Norwegian soil on 7th June 1945
after the Second World War.

showed admirable skill in keeping their households going, and
there was a general readiness to help. Unfortunately there were
also some, though only a few, who took advantage of the time
of want to acquire excessive earnings by selling commodities at
high prices on the black market.

In May 1945 the hour of liberation finally came. The German
army capitulated at several points on the European front, and
on May 7th the German High Command made an unconditional
surrender to the allied forces. This capitulation also included the
German forces stationed in Norway, and thus the Norwegians
were spared further hostilities on their own soil.

A wave of joy and gratitude swept through the Norwegian
people when the news came that their country was finally free
again. For several days people rejoiced without end and the
17th of May that year was celebrated by greater numbers and
with a greater ardour than ever before.

The climax of the liberation came on June 7th when King Haakon, after an absence of five years, returned to Norway and made his entry in the capital. The date had been selected both in memory of the sad 7th June in 1940 and of the joyful 7th of June in 1905. The King was welcomed with indescribable joy by huge crowds in the streets of Oslo, and throughout the whole country the return of the King was celebrated with enthusiasm and acclamation. It was an eloquent testimony to the deep respect and immense popularity Haakon VII had won through his wise and tactful conduct in the years of peace and his firm attitude in the crisis of 1940. For twelve more years he continued to reign, and after his death in 1957 he was succeeded by his son *Olav V*, who as Crown Prince had stood faithfully by his father's side in the years of trial.

9. *The Post-war Years.*

a. *Reconstruction and Economic Expansion.*

During the invasion of 1940, several towns and densely populated districts were destroyed by German bombing. When in the autumn of 1944 the Germans withdrew their troops from Finnmark and the northern half of the county of Troms, they destroyed nearly all houses, buildings, and harbour facilities in these areas.

An important task after the liberation was to rebuild the war-ravaged districts, and in addition it was necessary to set going an extensive house-building programme in the remainder of the country, especially in the large towns. During the five years of occupation no building had taken place, and this had brought about an acute housing shortage. The housing shortage was the most serious social problem of the post-war years.

This problem could not be solved rapidly, because there was also a shortage of essential building materials, such as bricks

130

and cement. There was, too, a shortage of manpower. An important task was to furnish new equipment and machines for factories, workshops, fisheries, and agriculture, since it was vital to get all industries started and modernise them. It was of special importance to rebuild the merchant marine. This was done in the space of four years, and in the years that followed the fleet increased in size and became much larger than before the war. In 1971 the fleet consisted of about 2,900 ships with a total of 21 million gross tons, which was nearly ten per cent of the world's merchant shipping. However, the oil crisis of 1973 has had a profound impact on the fleet, with several tankers being laid up and orders for new vessels being cancelled.

Industry also underwent a considerable expansion during the post-war period. Not only were existing industrial plants extended, but new ones were developed, often with Government aid or as Government projects. As a result of this expansion, unemployment has been practically non-existent in the post-war period. On the whole the period has been one of full employment and of general improvement in the standard of living of the Norwegian people.

The greatly intensified utilisation of waterfalls for electric power production has been of basic importance. With the aid of hydro-electricity, the output of a number of chemical and metallurgical products has reached levels many times as high as before the war. However, the nation's new resource — off-shore oil on the North Sea continental shelf — has since 1973 had an ever-increasing impact on the Norwegian economy.

At the same time production in agriculture has also increased, even though industry and development projects have absorbed tens of thousands of workers from agriculture. The increase has been made possible because farmers have begun more and more to adopt the methods of mechanised agriculture, with tractors and other machines. Although the population actively engaged in agriculture has decreased, the total area of land under cultivation has increased by 250,000 acres in the years 1939 to 1959.

131

Many people were afraid that reconstruction and economic expansion, combined with an abundant supply of money, would create inflation and perhaps lead to large deficits in the balance of payments abroad. The foreign aid received through the Marshall Plan (in all 2,500 million kroner) helped to avert these dangers to some extent. In addition, there was some restriction of imports. Through price control and subsidies it became possible to stabilise prices for a certain period. But after the Norwegian krone was devalued in 1949, price control and subsidies were either modified or abolished. This, together with the general rise of prices in the world market, caused the cost of living index to go up in the 1950's by more than 60 %. The rise has continued during the 1960's, although on a smaller scale.

The balance of payments showed a credit balance in some of the post-war years, and a deficit in others, at times quite large. But even after the Marshall Aid came to an end, the deficits were no larger than could be covered with the assistance of long-term foreign loans.

The question of price control and Government planning of economic life provoked considerable political strife. It created the main division between the parties. The Labour Party and the Communist Party were declared adherents of control and planning, with the Conservative Party clearly in opposition. An intermediate position was adopted by the other parties, the Liberals, the Farmers' Party (later known as the Centre Party), and the Christian People's Party, a party which had been promoted locally in the last elections before the war, but which received wider support throughout the nation after the war.

With regard to social policy, however, there was no basic disagreement. All parties supported the extension of legislation for labour protection and social insurance, and the general work of establishing a welfare state.

For the first few months after the liberation, Norway was ruled by a *coalition government*. But in the autumn elections of 1945 the Labour Party won an absolute majority in the Storting,

Einar Gerhardsen.   *Per Borten.*

and kept this majority at the next three elections. Consequently it has stayed in power during the post-war period. It lost its majority in the election of 1961, but was still by far the strongest party, and so continued in office. In 1961 the left wing of the Labour Party broke away and formed the *Socialist People's Party*, which stood for Norwegian disarmament and withdrawal from the NATO (see page 141). In the elections the party gained only 2 representatives, which was far out of proportion to its number of votes. The Communist Party lost the only representative it had by then. The general distribution of seats in the Storting for the period 1961 to 1965 was as follows: Labour 74, Socialist People's Party 2, Liberals 14, Centre 16, Christian People's Party 15, Conservatives 29.

The leaders of the Labour Party in the post-war years have been *Einar Gerhardsen* and *Oscar Torp* (who died in 1958), and both have been in office as Prime Minister. *Halvard Lange* has been Foreign Minister, with a brief interruption, from February, 1946 till Oct. 1965.

In August, 1963, there was a change of government after a dramatic Parliamentary debate provoked by a disaster that had happened in a state-owned mine in Svalbard. The opposition charged the Labour Government with not following certain security directions which had been given by the Storting several years before. The 2 representatives of the Socialist People's Party voted together with the 74 non-socialists in favour of a motion of no-confidence. Thereupon a coalition government was formed, consisting of members drawn from all four non-socialist parties (Conservatives, Liberals, Centre and Christian People's Party.) For the first time in 28 years Norway had a non-socialist premier.

However, the Government fell after less than a month, both the 74 Labour and the 2 Socialist People's Party members voting against it. It was replaced by a new Labour Government. After this rapid succession of governmental crises, caused by an awkward Parliamentary situation and the lack of a stable majority, the question of a constitutional amendment introducing the right of dissolving the Storting was taken up.

In the elections of September 1965 the non-socialist parties won an absolute majority in the Storting (80 seats out of 150) and again formed a coalition government. Per Borten of the Centre was made Prime Minister.

The elections of 1969 also gave a non-socialist majority (76 seats against 74), but in the course of the early months of 1971 it became clear that collaboration was getting more and more difficult between the four independent parties represented in the government. This was above all due to the rather reticent attitude taken by the Prime Minister and his party towards EEC negociations for full membership. A so-called leakage from Prime Minister Borten to the leader of the «People's Movement against the EEC» brought an end to the coalition government. After a fruitless attempt to set up a new non-socialist government, a minority government of the Labour Party was formed, with Trygve Bratteli as Prime Minister and Andreas Cappelen as Foreign Minister.

This government in January 1972 completed the negotiations with the EEC by signing a protocol of membership. In accordance with a previous decision, however, the question was submitted to a national referendum. After a heated campaign, marked by a degree of passion rare in Norwegian politics, the people on 25 September 1972 by a majority of 53.5 per cent turned down the proposed membership in the European Community — for various and complex reasons including the fear of seeing the autonomy of a small nation on Europe's periphery submerged.

Following the referendum, by which the people had also rejected the advice of the Labour party in favour of the treaty of membership, the Bratteli government resigned in favour of a minority coalition of the Centre party, the Christian People's party, and the remains of the Liberals. The new government, with Lars Korvald of the Christian People's party as Prime Minister, negotiated a trade agreement with the EEC which in July 1973 was unanimously ratified by the Storting. But the divisions of the "European issue" had a profound impact on the political stage. Before the elections of 1973 the Liberals were split in two, and a small group of the Labour party joined with the Socialist People's Party and the Communists in a Socialist Electoral Alliance. In addition, a right-wing grouping, namned after their leader as "Anders Lange's party for a strong reduction of taxes and of state intervention", competed for the favours of the electorate.

The results of the election confirmed the unsettling effects of the European question and its corollaries. Labour was returned with only 62 of the 155 representatives in the new Storting, and Trygve Bratteli's return as Prime Minister was only achieved with the support of the Socialist Electoral Alliance.

The principal tasks of the new Labour government soon turned out to be centred on oil, in two respects: First, to fashion a national policy for the exploitation of the huge off-shore oil resources of the North Sea, in a manner which would provide maximum benefits to all parts of the population while avoiding the "boom" conditions of an oil rush. Second, to manage the economy so as to dampen the effects of the international recession triggered by the sharply increased prices of Middle East oil.

The national oil policy, around which a wide consensus soon formed, built on two cornerstones: A strictly controlled, moderate pace of exploitation with a preponderant role assigned to the new State Oil Corporation; and a determination to avoid Norway becoming just an exporter of crude oil, which translated itself into extensive plans for a nationally based petro-chemical industry. At the same time, the economic activity engendered by the oil resources, and the deliberate acceptance of large foreign currency deficit on the promise of subsequent surpluses from the export of oil products, enabled Norway as the only western industrialised nation to maintain a marked rate of growth in its economy through the critical year of 1975. By the beginning of 1976 the unemployment rate had not yet exceeded the two per cent mark. The source of major concern remained the high inflation rate, which in 1975 touched 12 per cent. Hopes to combat this danger centred on intensified efforts to achieve a national incomes policy through cooperation between labour, management, and the government.

The moderate impact of the international recession on the Norwegian economy no doubt contributed to a return to normal politics after the upheavals of the EEC issue. The opinion polls, and the local elections of September 1975, suggested at least that the Labour party was regaining some of its lost strength. In this it may have been helped by the inability of the non-socialist opposition to forge a united front, and by the failure of the Socialist Electoral Alliance to transform itself into a unified political party. This failure became evident in the autumn of 1975 when the orthodox core of the Communist party refused to surrender its separate identity. One expression of the Labour party's regained strength was its success in effecting an orderly change of

136

leadership, as Trygve Bratteli relinquised his dual position as party chairman and Prime Minister to two men: Reiulf Steen, as party leader, and Odvar Nordli, who in January 1976 formed a new Labour minority government.

In March, 1981, Mr. Nordli resigned his office for reasons of health, and was replaced by Norway's first woman Prime Minister, the 41 years old medical doctor Gro Harlem Brundtland. She inherited from her predecessor an economy which, while it had managed to avoid the massive unemployment that beset most of the western world, thanks largely to the comfortable cushion provided by Norway's oil wealth, was suffering from declining productivity and a high inflation rate. Other than that, the Government faced the problem of trying to defuse the conflict over the construction of a hydroelectric power plant by the Alta river in North Norway. During the winter a sizable police force had had to remove hundreds of demonstrators who, under the dual banners of protection of the environment and defence of the rights of the Lapp minority of the region, had sat down in front of the bulldozers.

Although the fresh appeal of an energetic new leader managed to stem the decline of the Labour party in the opinion polls, it was not sufficient to prevent the three main non-Socialist parties from winning a majority of seats in the parliamentary elections in September 1981. And after a failed attempt to form a non-Socialist coalition government, Kaare Willoch formed the first Conservative government in Norway since 1928, with a declaration of support from the Agrarian and Christian People's parties. The new Prime Minister promised tax cuts but warned that public expenditure would have to be cut, as the country was living beyond its means.

b. *Defence and Peace Policies.*

The German attack on Norway in 1940 and the five ensuing years of occupation had made an indelible impression on the minds of the Norwegian people and had created a firm resolve to protect the freedom and independence of the nation. Consequently all political parties agreed after the war to build up a strong military defence, even if this meant sacrifices in the form of heavy taxation and long military service.

Immediately after the liberation, those who had collaborated with the Germans were brought to trial for treason. Thirty persons were condemned to death and twenty-five of them executed. Vidkun Quisling was among the latter. A substantial number were sentenced to imprisonment, while the majority only had to pay fines, some of them heavy. A total of about 500 persons were sentenced to as much as 8 years or more of prison, but practically all were released after a much shorter period. In 1957 the last of those who had received life sentences were pardoned. The trial of Quisling's adherents and of other collaborators concerned no more than about 2 per cent of the population, and their re-integration into society has therefore presented no great problem.

The one lasting effect of the war in internal Norwegian politics was the creation of a strong feeling of unity between all sections of the people. There is a striking contrast between the acute dissension and disagreement of the years between the two World Wars, and the confident atmosphere of mutual cooperation characteristic of the post-war years. At the 1945 general elections the parties agreed on a common programme of reconstruction policy, and although some divergencies have appeared later, they are only of minor importance when compared to the serious divisions of the inter-war years both between the parties and between different sectors of the population. No doubt this harmony is partly due to the general economic prosperity prevailing after the war, but the sentiment of unity developed during the five years of struggle against a common enemy certainly also played a great part in producing the striking change in political climate which is a main feature of recent Norwegian history.

In 1945 Norway became one of the founding members of the

United Nations Organisation (UNO). When entering the League of Nations in 1920, the country had acted in accordance with her traditional policy of supporting the forces that were in favour of world peace, but not in accordance with her other traditional policy of maintaining strict neutrality in conflicts among the great powers, since the Covenant foresaw the possibility that collective military action against one or more aggressor nations might be decided upon. Though their country did join the League, a great many Norwegians were loath to give up the idea of staying out of future great power conflicts. In the latter part of the 1930's it became abundantly clear that the League of Nations would not be able to prevent a second World War, and the Scandinavian states, Norway among them, declared that they reverted to their old policy of neutrality.

The German invasion of 1940 brought about a complete revaluation of Norwegian foreign policy. Halvdan Koht, Minister of Foreign Affairs since 1935, had been an ardent spokesman of neutrality. In the autumn of 1940 he was, as mentioned before, succeeded by Trygve Lie. Shortly afterwards, in a radio address, Lie squared accounts with the past, with neutrality, and with the isolationism that had played such an important part in Norwegian foreign affairs. It was no longer possible to stand alone, he said. In order to preserve the personal and national rights which Norwegians regarded as basic, the nation was obliged to work together with other free countries, especially those in the West, Great Britain and the United States. This was imperative not only for the liberation of Norway but also for the nation's future existence. Cultural and economic relations provided a solid foundation on which to build.

The German invasion of the USSR in June 1941 brought the Soviet Union into the war on the side of the Allies. In the autumn of 1941 Trygve Lie reiterated that regional cooperation with Great Britain and the USA must constitute the major premise of Norwegian foreign policy. But it was also important to remain on a neighbourly footing with the Soviet Union and, by means of a comprehensive international plan, to establish closer relations with other countries. These ideas were further developed in the summer of 1942 in a statement of principle approved both by the Government and by leaders of the resistance movement in occupied Norway. Certain points were doubtless affected by war-time conditions, but the statement clearly expressed the principles which were to determine Norwegian foreign policy after the war.

With the establishment of the United Nations Organisation, Norway was once again faced in principle with the choice between binding obligations to cooperate within an international security system and, on the other hand, neutral isolationism. It had fully experienced the price of standing alone. Considering the technical development of armaments during the war, prospects for the future appeared even more uncertain. No one in the committee of experts which studied the situation for the Government proposed that Norway should pursue a policy of isolationism.

One of the crucial paragraphs in the United Nations Charter provided for a Great Power veto. Norway voted in favour of this paragraph. If the organisation were to accomplish its aims, the Great Powers would necessarily have to follow the same policy. Should there be disagreement among them, it would be impossible to provide international security. The success or failure of the UNO was thus dependent upon continued cooperation between the Great Powers which had permanent seats in the Security Council. This determined the policy which Norway was to follow in the first post-war years, the so-called policy of bridge-building. During this period, Norway tried to contribute to the maintenance of harmony between the Great Powers.

Consideration for the future of the UNO was not the only argument in favour of conciliation. Norway's own position was an exposed one. A conflict between the Soviet Union and the Western Powers could easily make her northernmost provinces an area of strategic importance. For this reason, too, every possible endeavour must be made to help preserve mutually confident relations between East and West.

These political considerations were supported by a wave of pro-Russian sentiment. Most Norwegians were rightfully impressed by the achievements of the Russian forces during the war and particularly during the liberation of Finnmark, where the Russian troops showed excellent behaviour. It was also assumed that the USSR, which had suffered such great losses in population and material, would wish to return to the status quo and concentrate on reconstruction.

Nor must one neglect the traditional conception of Norway as a well-qualified mediator. There should be no reason to doubt the country's good faith towards both East and West. Having never had any disagreement with either party, Norway might be well suited to build a bridge between the power groups, if ideological or other factors should make mutual understanding difficult.

Trygve Lie was among those who gave whole-hearted support to the policy of conciliation and who counted on an easing of political tension over a long period, during which matters of security would recede in favour of economic and cultural cooperation. Norway had to be uncommitted in order to act as an intermediary and an arbitrator between the Great Powers. The creation of definite blocs would only tend to lessen the confidence which was a prerequisite for peaceful development. This impartial attitude was one of the reasons for Trygve Lie's election in 1946 as Secretary-General of the UNO. Halvard Lange, who succeeded Lie as Norwegian Minister of Foreign Affairs, shared his opinion. The country's task was to promote cooperation among all nations without joining any bloc. This policy was based on an evaluation of the state of world affairs in 1945—46.

The situation soon changed, however. Within the first year after the war the Soviet Union gained control of most of the small nations of eastern Europe. Each of these was formally joined to the USSR by agreements for mutual support. In practice this meant their loss of democratic rights and subordination to Russian interests. In both foreign and domestic policy they became dependent upon the Soviet Union.

This was contrary to the Allies' agreement of 1945, and aroused suspicion that the Soviet Union was consciously engaged upon a policy of expanding its influence throughout the non-Russian portion of Europe. Events in Greece, the Russian attitude towards the German question and the establishment of the *Cominform*[1]) served to strengthen this point of view. In the summer of 1947 the Americans declared that they would contribute actively, under the Marshall Plan, to the work of reconstruction in Europe. About the same time, American military guarantees and economic support were given to Greece and Turkey. Tension mounted steadily and reached a climax when, in February 1948, Czechoslovakia was also drawn behind what was now coming to be known as the "iron curtain".

The coup d'état in Czechoslovakia was the turning-point in Norwegian policy on national security. It led to the renunciation of the policy of mediation. Czechoslovakia occupied an exceptional place in Norwegian public opinion, and especially the death in March of the Foreign Minister, *Jan Masaryk*, made a profound impression. Russian pressure on Finland strengthened the impression of imminent danger.

The emergence of two opposed blocs and the Soviet Union's frequent use of the veto indicated that the conflict of interests between East and West could not be mitigated by benevolent arbitrator nations. Soviet policy gave rise to fears that other small, neighbouring countries might lose their independence. Meanwhile, it had been realised that the UNO by itself was unable to guarantee the security of its members. This evaluation raised a question of vital importance: — Could Norway, under the new

[1])*Communist Information Bureau*, a revival of the *Communist International*, which had been dissolved in 1943.

circumstances, reach security by intensified rearmament at the expense of many of her plans for economic development? Or would it be necessary to accept aid from abroad in order to bring Norwegian security measures into balance?

In theory, the country was faced once again with the choice between neutral isolationism and international solidarity, but the alternatives were no longer so clearly defined as before. Theoretically there were four possibilites: 1) to remain neutral and isolationist; 2) to join a neutral Scandinavian defensive alliance; 3) to join a Scandinavian alliance linked with the West; 4) to join an Atlantic defensive alliance.

In the autumn of 1948 negotiations were started between Sweden, Denmark and Norway with a view to settling the conditions of a Scandinavian alliance. The question of rearmament and of military aid from outside was discussed. The Norwegian representatives maintained that, even if all three countries did their very best, they would be unable to provide Scandinavia with sufficient protection unless they sought help from abroad. If this were to be effective, it would have to be accomplished in peacetime by working closely together with the Great Powers in the West. A completely neutral alliance would not satisfy the requirements for security.

Sweden, however, having stayed neutral during both World Wars, decided to continue its old policy. The outcome of the Scandinavian discussions being negative, Norway and Denmark decided to open negotiations with the Western Powers. In February, 1949, the Norwegian government sent a delegation to Washington to obtain information about the plans for common defence which were being discussed between representatives of the USA, Canada, Great Britain, France, and the Benelux countries.

Pressure from Russia to some extent influenced the Norwegian attitude. On January 29th, 1949, the Russian ambassador delivered a note with a Soviet warning against the Atlantic pact. The USSR demanded to know whether Norway intended to join and to what extent it had agreed to open naval or air force bases on its territory. In its reply of February 1st, the Norwegian Government stated that it would investigate conditions of membership in the Western defence union but that it would not permit the establishment of bases "unless Norway were attacked or exposed to threats of attack". The Russians were not satisfied with the answer, and in a new note of February 5th, the Soviet Union requested further assurance and invited Norway to conclude a treaty of non-aggression. The Government's reply, which was made some weeks later, rejected the offer but confirmed the reservation concerning bases, a reservation which has since been maintained.

Faced with pressure from outside, with the economic need to rebuild, and with the certain realisation that Norway was open and practically without defence, the nation was obliged to decide finally which course it would follow. Especially within the party in power many were hesitant concerning cooperation with the West, but they also recognised existing dangers and the difficulty of finding a reliable alternative. At its national convention on February 19th, 1949, the Labour Party, after first voting 329 against 35, finally decided unanimously in favour of joining the West. On March 3rd, the Storting approved the idea of membership, and Norway participated in the final formulation of the agreement, which was completed around the middle of the month. On March 29th the Storting ratified Norwegian membership in the North Atlantic Treaty Organisation by 130 votes against 13 (11 Communist and 2 Labour Party Members). Norwegian foreign policy was thus once again brought in line with the principles established in 1942.

At the close of the Scandinavian defence negotiations in January, 1949, the three Governments declared that, even if they were not in agreement on the question of military security, they would continue to work together in other ways. In fact, since 1949 there has been a steady development of the cultural, social, and various other ties which unite these countries. The Scandinavian Ministers of Foreign Affairs still meet regularly, and the Goverments are in continual contact. Delegations from the three countries usually work closely with each other in most organisations where they are members. The fact that Sweden follows a policy of neutrality, whereas Norway and Denmark are allied in the NATO, has had suprisingly little effect upon their attitude to international cooperation. Usually they maintain a common policy. (Their contribution to the UNO police force in Gaza and the Congo has also helped to increase the feeling of solidarity.)

There are so many ties between these nations, cultural, linguistic, political, and social. Geography, too, has forced upon them a common destiny which is unavoidable. What happens to one must necessarily affect the others. This had led many to conclude that there might evolve some sort of a United States of Scandinavia. The idea opens wide perspectives for the future, but that future is probably very distant. In Norwegian quarters there still prevails the view which was expressed in 1941—42 and which was the major point during negotiations for a Scandinavian defensive alliance: an isolated Scandinavian unit would rest upon far too unstable a foundation, economically as well as in matters of defence. On the other hand, closer cooperation among neighbouring nations in practical matters is advantageous within a wider international framework.

The formation of the Nordic Council in 1952, with Denmark, Iceland, Finland, Sweden and Norway as members, was a step in this direction. Not only has it provided a common forum for members of the Scandinavian parliaments and governments. It has also put into practice a long series of concrete measures which have helped to increase understanding and solidarity among these countries. On the recommendation of the Nordic Council, the member countries have introduced joint customs inspection, abolition of passport requirements, and parallel legislation within certain areas of law. The Cultural Affairs Commission has performed a valuable task in coordinating university standards, arranging joint research programmes, etc. In certain fields great progress has been made in common scientific projects. In welfare measures much work has been done on joint insurance programmes and other social benefits. Since 1954 there has been a common labour market.

On several occasions during the postwar period, the Nordic countries had explored the possibilities of a customs union or a common market arrangement, but without success, for a multitude of reasons including those stemming from differences of foreign policy or of economic orientation and structure. At the same time, all the four countries have sought to obtain the benefits of access to the larger European market, through EFTA or the European Free Trade Area, and for a short time through a planned fusion between EFTA and the Common Market. When this latter project failed, however, it was up to each country to determine its own relationship with the European Community. During this process, the paths of the Nordic countries separated. Finland and Sweden felt constrained by their neutrality to opt for a strictly commercial relationsship. But for Norway, as for Denmark, the alternative of full membership was a possibility to be fully considered.

For two years a heated debate raged which engaged all sections of the Norwegian public. Economically the advantages to be gained from full membership appeared considerable, even when mingled with apprehensions as to the future prospects of Norwegian agriculture in open competition with geographically and climatically more advantageous areas. On the political front, fears centred on seeing the autonomy of a small country eroded through the concentration of power on the Continent.

The final decision was taken by a popular referendum on 25 September 1972. With the fairly narrow margin of 53.5 per cent, the nation rejected membership in the European Community. Thereafter, Norway negotiated a commercial treaty with the Common Market which took into account the very strong economic links which inevitably must exist between Norway and her European neighbours.

Generally speaking, Norway has traditionally been in favour of

146

free world trade, both because of the large part played by foreign trade in the country's economy, and on account of the interests of her merchant navy. In later years, however, public debate in Norway has paid increasing attention to the needs of the developing countries for preferential arrangements which go against the trend towards trade liberalisation.

As a member of the United Nations Norway has made annual contributions to the work of helping the underdeveloped countries. But in this field Norway has also set on foot a project of her own to aid a province in India. Through Government grants and private subscriptions a fund has been raised for the development of the fishing industry in Kerala (Travancore-Cochin) on the south-western coast of India under the guidance of Norwegian experts.

Norway is playing an active part in the North-South relations. Official development aid (ODA) in 1978 reached the UN target of 1 per cent of the Gross National Product (GNP). Allocations are divided equally between multilateral aid, mainly through the UN, and bilateral aid. All aid is given as free grants and is in principle untied. Bilateral aid is for a greater part concentrated to 9 main partner countries, India, Bangladesh, Pakistan and Sri Lanka in Asia, and Kenya, Tanzania, Zambia, Botswana, and Mozambique in Africa. Substantial development assistance has also been given to Vietnam, Indonesia, and Portugal.

Norway is also encouraging commercial relations with the developing countries and has adopted a series of measures to facilitate the access to the Norwegian market for the products of these countries. Similar measures have been adopted to encourage investments in and exports to the third world countries. Norway is also known as a staunch supporter of the demand for a new international economic order giving the poor countries a fairer deal in the global economic relations.

Equally important for the future, however, is the avoidance of major military conflicts between nations and the limitation of armaments, both atomic and conventional. The Norwegian Government has decided not to accept atomic weapons on her

147

territory in·time of peace. And in accordance with this policy it has supported the agreement made in 1963 between the United States, the Soviet Union and Great Britain imposing a partial ban on nuclear tests. However, Norway in December 1979 joined the other NATO countries in deciding to deploy intermediate range nuclear weapons in Europe by 1983 unless an agreement could be reached limiting the massive Soviet deployment of such weapons. Also, Norway decided to counter the threat of encirclement by the expanding Soviet naval strength in the north by concluding agreements providing for the pre-positioning of arms and equipment for American and Canadian reinforcements. On the other hand, in its last year in office the Labour government lent its support to the growing grass-roots campaign against nuclear weapons, and agreed to work for a nuclear-free zone in the Nordic area. But the Conservative government which took office in October 1981 stressed the need for western solidarity and for a mutual and balanced disarmament process. It also increased the defence budget by four instead of the three percent proposed by the outgoing Labour government.

In Norwegian eyes the United Nations Organisation provides important possibilities for contact and peaceful settlement of international disputes. In this field Norway has tried to carry on her traditional policy of preserving peace. The country has taken part in a number of international schemes during the post-war period. Her troops have served with the United Nations Gaza Patrol in the Near East and with the security forces which were sent to the Congo during the disturbances there. In May 1978 a Norwegian battalion – together with a medical company, a maintenance company, and a helicopter wing – was sent to South Lebanon as part of the United Nations' Interim Force in Lebanon to help maintain the truce between Israel and the P.L.O.

Thus in our time the descendants of the vikings go to remote countries to assist in promoting prosperity, restoring order, and securing peace.

148

A. Kings of Norway circa 900—1380.

Harald Fairhair (Harald I)	circa 900 — 940
Erik Bloodaxe (Erik I)	» 940 — 945
Haakon the Good (Haakon I)	» 945 — 960
Harald Graypelt (Harald II)	» 960 — 970
Earl Haakon	» 970 — 995
Olav Tryggvason (Olav I)	995 — 1000
Earls Erik and Svein	1000 — 1016
Olav Haraldson (St. Olav, Olav II)	1016 — 1030
Canute the Great (Prince Svein Alfivason regent)	1030 — 1035
Magnus the Good (Magnus I)	1035 — 1047
Harald Hardrade (Harald III)	1047 — 1066
Olav the Peaceful (Olav III)	1066 — 1093
Magnus Bareleg (Magnus II)	1093 — 1103
Eystein Magnusson (Eystein I)	1103 — 1125
Sigurd Magnusson the Crusader (Sigurd I)	1103 — 1130
Harald Gilchrist (Harald IV)	1130 — 1136
Magnus Sigurdson the Blind (Magnus III)	1130 — 1138
Inge Haraldson (Inge I)	
Sigurd Haraldson (Sigurd II)	1136 — 1161
Eystein Haraldson (Eystein II)	
Haakon Sigurdson (Haakon II)	1161 — 1162
Magnus Erlingson (Magnus IV)	1163 — 1184
Sverre Sigurdson	1184 — 1202
Haakon Sverreson (Haakon III)	1202 — 1204
Inge Baardson (Inge II)	1204 — 1217
Haakon Haakonson (Haakon IV)	1217 — 1263
Magnus Haakonson the Lawmender (Magnus V)	1263 — 1280
Erik Magnusson (Erik II)	1280 — 1299
Haakon Magnusson (Haakon V)	1299 — 1319
Magnus Erikson (Magnus VI)	1319 — 1355
(Personal union with Sweden)	
Haakon Magnusson (Haakon VI)	1355 — 1380

B. Kings of Denmark and Norway 1380—1814.

Olav Haakonson (Olav IV)	1380 — 1387
Queen Margaret	1387 — 1412
Erik of Pomerania (Erik III)	1389 — 1442
Christopher of Bavaria	1442 — 1448
Christian I	1448 — 1481
Hans	1481 — 1513
Christian II	1513 — 1523
Frederik I	1523 — 1533
Christian III	1537 — 1559
Frederik II	1559 — 1588
Christian IV	1588 — 1648
Frederik III	1648. — 1670
Christian V	1670 — 1699
Frederik IV	1699 — 1730
Christian VI	1730 — 1746
Frederik V	1746 — 1766
Christian VII	1766 — 1808
Frederik VI	1808 — 1814

Christian Frederik, King of Norway 17th May—4th November 1814

C. Kings of Sweden and Norway 1814—1905.

Carl XIII	1814 — 1818
Carl Johan (Bernadotte)	1818 — 1844
Oscar I	1844 — 1859
Carl XV	1859 — 1872
Oscar II	1872 — 1905

D. Kings of Norway since 1905.

Haakon VII	1905 — 1957
Olav V	1957 —

LEADERS OF THE NORWEGIAN GOVERNMENT
1814—1981

Prior to 1884, Norwegian Government members were chosen by the King on a non-party basis. Most of them were conservative in outlook. The office of Prime Minister was not instituted till 1873. In the following list, the men commonly thought to be most influential in the Government are regarded as leaders prior to 1873, and the Prime Ministers are listed from then onwards. The party basis of governments is given from 1884:

1814 — 1822:	Count J. C. H. *Wedel Jarlsberg*
1822 — 1858	Jonas *Collett*
	Count J. C. H. *Wedel Jarlsberg*
	Severin *Løvenskiold*
	Jørgen Herman *Vogt*
1858 — 1861:	Chr. *Birch-Reichenwald*
1861 — 1880:	Frederik *Stang*
1880 — 1884:	Chr. Aug. *Selmer*
April — June 1884:	Chr. *Schweigaard*
1884 — 1889:	Johan *Sverdrup*, Liberal
1889 — 1891:	Emil *Stang*, Conservative
1891 — 1893:	Johannes *Steen*, Liberal
1893 — 1895:	Emil *Stang*, Conservative
1895 — 1898:	Francis *Hagerup*, Coalition
1898 — 1902:	Johannes *Steen*, Liberal
1902 — 1903:	Otto *Blehr*, Liberal
1903 — 1905:	Francis *Hagerup*, Conservative
1905 — 1907:	Christian *Michelsen*, Coalition
1907 — 1908:	J. *Løvland*,Moderate Liberal
1908 — 1910:	Gunnar *Knudsen*, Liberal
1910 — 1912:	Wollert *Konow*, Conservative
1912 — 1913:	Jens *Bratlie*, Conservative
1913 — 1920:	Gunnar *Knudsen*, Liberal
1920 — 1921:	Otto B. *Halvorsen*, Conservative

1921 — 1923:	Otto *Blehr*, Liberal
March — May 1923:	Otto B. *Halvorsen*, Conservative
1923 — 1924:	Abraham *Berge*, Conservative
1924 — 1926:	Johan L. *Mowinckel*, Liberal
1926 — 1928:	Ivar *Lykke*, Conservative
January — February 1928:	Christopher *Hornsrud*, Labour
1928 — 1931:	Johan L. *Mowinckel*, Liberal
1931 — 1932:	P. L. *Kolstad*, Agrarian
1932 — 1933:	Jens *Hundseid*, Agrarian
1933 — 1935:	Johan L. *Mowinckel*, Liberal
1935 — 1945:	Johan *Nygaardsvold*, Labour
1945 — 1951:	Einar *Gerhardsen*, Labour
1951 — 1955:	Oscar *Torp*, Labour
1955 — Aug. 1963:	Einar *Gerhardsen*, Labour
August 1963 — September 1963:	John *Lyng*, Coalition (Conservative / Liberal / Centre / Christian People's Party).
September 1963 — October 1965:	Einar *Gerhardsen*, Labour
October 1965 —	Per *Borten*, Coalition (same as in 1963).
March 1971 — October 1972	Trygve *Bratteli*. Labour
October 1972 — October 1973	Lars *Korvald*, Coalition (Christian People's Party, Centre / Liberals)
October 1973 — January 1976	Trygve *Bratteli*, Labour
January 1976 — March 1981	Odvar *Norli*, Labour
March 1981 — September 1981	Gro *Harlem Brundtland*, Labour
September 1981 —	Kaare *Willoch*, Conservative

152

1. General surveys.

K. Gjerset: A History of the Norwegian People. 2 vols. New York, 1915
H. Koht and S. Skard: The Voice of Norway, London and New York, 1944
W. Keilhau: Norway in World History, London, 1944
K. Larsen: A History of Norway, New York, 1948
T. K. Derry: A Short History of Norway, London 1957 (with a comprehensive bibliography)

2. Viking Age and Medieval Times.

The Cambridge Medieval History, Cambridge 1924
T. P. Kendrick: A History of the Vikings, London, 1930
A. W. Brøgger and H. Shetelig: The Viking Ships, Oslo, 1951
G. M. Gathorne-Hardy: The Norse Discoveries of America, Oxford 1921
H. Hermansson: The Problem of Wineland, Ithaca, New York 1936
G. M. Gathorne-Hardy: A Royal Impostor: King Sverre of Norway, Oslo and Oxford 1956, .
Heimskringla (Snorre Sturlasons Saga-book, translated by E. Monsen and A. H. Smith), Cambridge, 1932
The Saga of King Sverre, translated by J. Sephton, London 1899

3. Modern Times.

B. J. Hovde: The Scandinavian Countries 1720—1865, The Rise of the Middle Classes. 2 vols. Boston, Mass., 1943.
T. Jorgensen: Norway's Relations to Scandinavian Unionism 1815—1871, Northfield Minnesota, 1935
I. C. Blegen: The Norwegian Migration to America, 1825—60, Northfield, Minnesota 1931
Fridtjof Nansen: The Voyage of the Fram, London, 1897
J. Sorensen: The Saga of Fridtjof Nansen, New York, 1932
H. Koht: Norway Neutral and Invaded, London 1941
J. Worm-Müller: Norway revolts against the Nazis, London, 1941
T. K. Derry: The Campaign in Norway, London 1952.
Sten Sparre Nilson: Myth of the Fifth Column. The Norseman. Oslo. 1963 No. 1.

LIST OF VIGNETTES

Page 12: Prehistoric rock carving.

Page 20: Grotesque wooden head from the Oseberg find.

Page 45: King Eystein. Fragment of a statue from Munkeliv Monastery, Bergen. This is the first known portrait in Norwegian art.

154

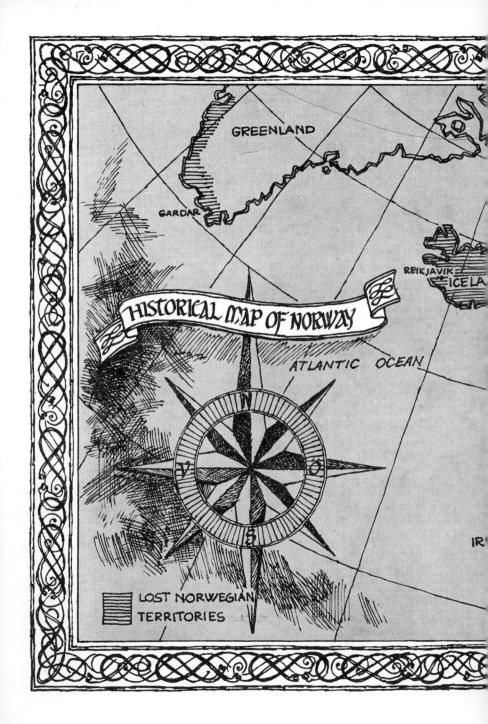